AWAKEN
YOUR
INNER GIFTS

Scott,
you ARE the
Gift mister~

M

Nov 07/16

Canadian Cataloguing First Publication Date: May 2014

ISBN 10: 1499674015   ISBN 13: 9781499674019

Dave Wali Waugh, RPC; Michael Talbot Kelly, MA, RCC; Peter Cheung; Rebecca Cheung; and Anne Marie Konas

AWAKEN YOUR INNER GIFTS

1. Spiritual Growth   2. Personal Development

Layout, design, typography and cover design by Lee Johnson
Book enabled by Lee Johnson : Literary Consultant, Ghostwriter and Editor

AWAKEN YOUR INNER GIFTS

A Map for Living with Greater Wellness, Joy, Fulfillment, Meaning and Purpose

DAVE WALI WAUGH, RPC

MICHAEL TALBOT KELLY, MA, RCC

PETER CHEUNG

REBECCA CHEUNG

ANNE MARIE KONAS

INTRODUCTION ·

*'Be grateful for whoever comes, because each
has been sent as a gift from beyond.'*

Rumi

*N*atural Gifts are innate resources within each of us. When we give these Gifts to meet a meaningful need in the world, we live with more joy and a deep sense of meaning and purpose.

Each of us is born with the seeds of these Natural Gifts within us. However, many people are not aware of their existence... and so these seeds lie dormant and unfulfilled.

Wholistic psychotherapists Dave Wali Waugh and Michael Talbot Kelly have been friends and mentors for over twenty years. Over the last decade, they noticed that more and more people were seeking their services because they felt an overwhelming lack of fulfillment and meaning in their lives. Many seemed lost and had no sense of purpose. These individuals' ages ranged from their early 20's to their late 50's, indicating that there was unrest in both the young and the middle aged. However, when these folks discovered their Natural Gifts and found a meaningful outlet to display their Gifts, they led totally different lives; ones filled with greater wellness, joy, fulfillment, meaning and purpose.

The changes were so drastic in these people's lives that Dave and Michael knew they had stumbled onto something significant. Thus, they wondered how they could collaborate to help more people heal from this suffering, to find their Natural Gifts.

One day while conversing over lunch, they both realized that they loved their lives and loved their work. In other words, they were living with the joy of 'meaning and purpose'. They felt blessed to bring their souls to what had become their calling and vocation. Between them, they possess Natural Gifts such as Spiritual Awareness, Facilitation, Encouragement, Teaching, Knowledge, Leadership and Healing, among others.

They realized at that moment that what they really had to offer other people was a kind of 'map'—a method to attain what they were both experiencing on a daily basis: a life full of fulfillment, meaning and purpose.

Michael and Dave were both busy with their private practices, but felt there was an innate need in the world to help others become aware of this map. They came up with a vision to form a Non-Profit Society to help others heal and identify their Natural Gifts so that they too could live on purpose and 'love their life'. Before long they decided to invite some friends who were passionate about the same things, and together they formed the Natural Gifts Society, with a mission to assist in the awakening of one's Natural Gifts so that each of us can live with more wellness, joy, passion, fulfillment, meaning and purpose.

One of the primary intents of the Society is to help young people discover their gifts early in life, and to enrich them by finding their unique paths. The Society has programs that also serve those in their mid-life and elder years to deal effectively and gracefully with life's challenges.

The Society's vision is to create a network of Natural Gift Centers around the world, beginning in Vancouver BC, from which they can deliver out-reach educational programs and develop supportive communities for those who are awakening to their Natural Gifts.

Historically, the notion of being born with innate gifts is seen in many of the world's wisdom traditions. In the Jewish tradition, gifts are referred to as *Divine Sparks*. In the Christian tradition they are referred to as *Spiritual Gifts*. Inner Gifts are also referred to in the Islamic and Sufi traditions as essential to give in order to fulfill your life purpose. In the First Nations tradition, gifts are seen as *'gifts from the Creator'* and referred to as *'discovering one's particular medicine'* that is necessary to give to others for living one's unique purpose or destiny. We have decided to refer to inner gifts as 'Natural Gifts' to honour the essence of all Traditions. These Natural Gifts are part of our True Nature.

The 'map' we have developed is intended to help orient people in this discovery process, and it can be expressed by the following equation:

$$MAP = TN + EQ + NG - PR + MN$$

For the joy of more MAP (Meaning And Purpose), rest into your TN (True Nature), discover your EQ (Essential Qualities) and NG (Natural Gifts), clear any PR (Personality Resistances), and give your gifts to a MN (Meaningful Need) you see in the world.

We hope you will enjoy the discovery of your own MAP.

Dave Wali Waugh, RPC

Michael Talbot Kelly, MA, RCC

Peter Cheung

Rebecca Cheung

Anne Marie Konas

Natural Gifts Society,
Vancouver, British Columbia, Canada
April 2014

"The meaning of life is to find your gift.

The purpose of life is to give it away."

— Pablo Picasso

INDEX

Page

CHAPTER 1:

NATURAL GIFTS— HOW TO ATTAIN MORE MEANING AND PURPOSE IN LIFE

Do you love your life? Do you love your work? Are you feeling joy in what you do? Are you feeling content and fulfilled? Does your work make a difference in someone's life or in the world in some meaningful way?

When we meet people who are on purpose with their life they most often say, "*I love my work. It doesn't seem like work. I can't believe I'm getting paid to do what I love. I feel so blessed!*"

When people are living with meaning and purpose, they often say, "*I love my life!*"

Such people are fortunate to get paid for doing what they love, and we would say their work becomes their calling or vocation. We believe it's a way of bringing your *soul* or *deeper self* to work. And—since we usually spend so much of our time at work—this creates a very practical form of spirituality. You don't necessarily have to be religious to be spiritual!

Then there are some people who have a job that pays the bills, or those who no longer need to work to make a living, but still feel on purpose through volunteering or being creative. Being on purpose—doing what you love just for the love of it—we would call this 'following your avocation'. Perhaps, someday, it might even become your vocation.

The famous poet T.S. Elliot suffered physical disabilities as a boy, and so he channeled his creative gifts into reading and writing. As an adult he worked for a time as a teacher and later at a publishing house that published other poets. He often had to take uninteresting jobs to pay the bills, but still found a place for his Natural Gifts of teaching and writing.

One of his most famous quotes helps point us in the right direction:

"We shall not cease from exploration, and the end of all our exploring will be to arrive where we started and know the place for the first time."

When you awaken your Natural Gifts and give them to a meaningful need you see in the world, you will feel greater joy, fulfillment, meaning and purpose.

T.S. Elliot discovered that the Source of his gift came from deep inside of himself. We would call this his True Nature (TN). Our True Nature is like a great fountain out of which the water of Essential Qualities (EQ) flow, such as patience, love, compassion, awareness, presence, truth, kindness, forgiveness, courage, and so forth.

Each day we are given a choice. Are we going to be yanked by the chain of our ego/personality to go in the direction of the status quo? Or do we choose to remember our True Nature and receive our Essential Qualities and Natural Gifts so we can orient toward the life of purpose we love?

Are you feeling bored or exhausted at work? Are you wondering what your unique life purpose is?

In our map, we refer to this as Personality Resistance (PR). Our personality forms to protect us and to ensure we get our needs met.

It is often referred to as the *false self* or the *limited self* in spiritual traditions; nevertheless, it is healthy to have an ego/personality but it can block us from experiencing our True Nature and getting access to our Essential Qualities and Natural Gifts.

If you are presently feeling blocked, then the following pages may help you understand how to move through your blocks and to re-orient toward identifying and giving your gifts for greater joy, meaning and purpose.

AWAKENING YOUR GIFTS

There are many different ways people learn and many ways that you can awaken your Natural Gifts.

Some people explore volunteering, watching films or reading books to find what sparks an awakening.

Some people like to work with a mentor to explore their inner landscape.

Some like to take tests to discover their Gifts. If you are one of these people, we have a Natural Gifts Assessment available on our website at *www.naturalgiftssociety.org* where you can begin the process of working with a Natural Gifts Guide or Natural Gifts Mentor to help uncover your Gifts.

Many people discover their Natural Gifts but then either forget them, or lack the Essential Qualities to manifest their Natural Gifts into the world. One of the ways to address this is through meditation.

There are enormous benefits in practicing regular meditation, including remembering one's True Nature, Essential Qualities and Natural Gifts.

Meditation is designed to gently ease through our limited self into our Unlimited Self to receive our inner resources for each day.

There are many different types of meditations, depending on your unique learning style.

AWARENESS MEDITATION

Let's begin with a basic expanding awareness meditation.

First, find a quiet place and give yourself enough time so you will be free of any major distractions. Then, find a comfortable position for your body.

Once you have learned this meditation, you'll probably close your eyes during the process... but for now, we suggest you read this line by line, and then close your eyes while you do that specific part of the meditation.

You could also record it and play the recording back to yourself, or check out our website for a recording.

BECOMING AWARE OF YOUR GIFTS

To begin with, it is helpful to state your intention so that you have focus and purpose for devoting your time to this practice. For example, '*May I rest in my True Nature so that my Inner Gifts awaken; gifts that I may give to the world and thus live with greater meaning and purpose for the highest good of all.*'

Begin noticing your thoughts, but try not to identify with them. Notice there are thoughts, and also space between the thoughts ... be aware of sounds around you and inside you, while also being aware of the silence.

Start to notice the first inner gift, the *gift of life*. Just notice that you have this gift of life coursing through your body. Be present to this great gift of life, and notice how it somehow responds to your attention.

Next, notice the great *gift of breath*. Become aware of each breath as it enters your body and then is released from your body.

Just notice the breath coming in, going out; coming in, going out. Notice this great gift of breath, and how there is nothing you have to consciously do to receive it.

Now, just for fun, imagine a reverse perspective on this process. Instead of thinking, '*I am breathing in*', on your next in-breath, imagine that the Universe is breathing out, and into you.

And instead of thinking, '*I am breathing out*', on your next out-breath, imagine the Universe is breathing in, drawing the breath out of your body.

Our True Nature is like this one Universal breath.

It breathes everybody and everything—all the trees, the flowers, the creatures. It doesn't discriminate.

It breathes everything ... and everyone.

THE GIFT OF YOUR BODY AND YOUR SENSES

Now notice the great gift of *your body*.

Become aware that this body is a vehicle for this breath. Contemplate the mystery of how your body is an extraordinarily complex organism that functions quite miraculously on its own in each moment of your life.

Now notice the gift of *your senses.*

Let's begin with the *gift of sight.* Even if your eyes are closed, you can notice the light streaming through your eyelids. You might see some inner images. Be aware of this gift of outer seeing—if your eyes are open—and the gift of insight, if your eyes are closed.

Now, just like an inner compass, shift your attention over to the *gift of hearing.*

You may hear yourself reading to yourself. Notice that there is sound, and then there is silence. Sometimes we focus on sound, and we miss the silence. But the words wouldn't even make sense without the silence—we need the pauses between the words.

Now focus your attention and move your awareness to the *gift of smell.*

This helps you to focus your attention and come into the present moment. Notice if there are any scents around you. Be aware of scent and notice that it comes and goes.

Now shift your attention to the *gift of taste.* Notice if you're thirsty, notice where that sensation is in your body. Feel gratitude for the gift of taste.

Now shift your attention to the *gift of touch.* Notice your back touching the chair, your hands touching your lap, and your feet touching the floor. Put all your attention on the sense of touch. Notice your awareness drop to your feet. Feel gratitude for the gift of touch.

SIXTH SENSE

Now let's move to the sixth sense, the *gift of inner body sensation.*

Shift your attention inside your body, moving your awareness up into the top of your head. See if you can send the intention for your scalp to relax.

Now move your awareness down from your scalp to your forehead, to your cheeks and jaw muscles. Go down to the back of your head, and notice if there's any tension in these areas ... and allow them to relax.

Move down to your neck, your shoulders, your arms and into your hands. Then bring your awareness to your chest, down your back and into your spine.

Now move your awareness down your spine to the center of your back, and then to the base of your spine. Move your attention to your belly and try to soften it.

Now move down to your hips, your thighs, your knees, and your calves ... and then all the way down into your feet. Just allow your feet to relax for a few moments.

Now let your whole body relax ... as if you could just send your energy right through the floor.

With every out-breath, imagine you could let your energy drop down into roots descending into the earth ...

helping you come into this present moment, rooted in this place.

Now, with the out-breath you can release anything you don't want to carry down into the earth. See if you can just let the breath and your awareness descend, letting it go down into the Earth.

Then with every in-breath, imagine you can bring vitality up through the roots, like shoots coming up. Feel that energy move into your feet and up into your legs.

Feel each in-breath bringing that energy up into the base of your spine. Feel that energy from the Earth coming up your body; feel that magnetism revitalizing you.

Bring it up into your belly area, and then up into your solar plexus. Then see if you can move it right into the center of your chest and into your heart center. This is like the center of a compass.

Imagine if you could go deeper into the center of your deep heart. This is a portal to your True Nature.

ESSENTIAL QUALITIES & NATURAL GIFTS

From this deep well, our essential qualities emerge— qualities such as compassion, courage, love, truth, patience, forgiveness, and so forth.

And from this same Source emerge our Natural Gifts— such as the gift of hospitality, the gift of compassion, and the gift of teaching. These gifts are meant to be gifts to the world that we steward on behalf of our True Nature.

Now, if it feels appropriate, feel gratitude for whatever came to you in this brief meditation you have just experienced. Perhaps it's gratitude for the shift from your personality to your Deep Self, into your True Nature ... now see if you can touch base with some of the gifts that you have been given.

You might wish to contemplate the meaningful need you'd like to give your gifts to.

For example, if you had the gift of teaching, what other gifts would you share? What lessons would you teach? And to whom?

Just sit in silence for a few moments more. Breathe deeply and evenly. Notice that you are more relaxed.

Now, start to bring your attention to your body again. When you have awareness of that, gently start to move your body, just enjoying being embodied.

At this point, you may enjoy stretching a bit as you complete your meditation.

Breathe deeply and evenly, feeling completely natural and relaxed.

That's it!

If you enjoyed this basic awareness meditation, you can find more on our website at www.Naturalgiftssociety.org.

SETTING THE TONE

This meditation was designed to give you a taste of one of the ways that we can get access to what we're trying to find words to speak about—our Natural Gifts. For some, it can be a really deep experience.

But, just as there are many different kinds of people, there are also many different ways to awaken your inner gifts. A good starting point is realizing how important it is to simply *be grateful.*

Most people who do this meditation gain an enhanced appreciation for the gift of life, the gift of breath, of their body, and the gift of all their senses. And each time you go deeper, you may discover even more inner or natural gifts.

Life is such a gift; such a blessing, and so easy to take for granted. That's why it's important to express our gratitude every single day.

"Want to be happy? Be grateful!" says Benedictine monk and author Brother David Stendl-Rast.

This meditation is important because it also holds the essence of what this book is about.

THE MAP TO DISCOVERING YOUR M.A.P.

For those who want to delve deeper into the psychology behind our map, we recommend reading James Hillman's book *The Soul's Code: In Search of Character and Calling.*

THE ACORN CONCEPT

Hillman introduces the idea that we are all born with a unique, formed soul already within us—a soul that shapes us as much as it is shaped by external factors and circumstances.

While this is not a new concept, the idea that we are in some way predisposed or destined—that each of us already has a uniqueness that is our 'calling'—is normally rejected by our culture. This rejection can find us living an unhappy fate.

How do we transform our fate into our destiny? This concept is described by Hillman as the *acorn myth*. In an interview, he describes it as follows:

"It is a worldwide myth in which each person comes into the world with something to do and to be. The myth says we enter the world with a calling."

In essence, the acorn theory expresses that unique something that you are; that you have; that has your best interests at its heart.

Unfortunately, our culture clings stubbornly to the 'Nature-Nurture' theory, implying that you come into the world with a basic set of genes and are subsequently influenced by nature, by the environment, by parents, family, social class and education.

Problem is, these theories do not embrace the individuality and uniqueness that you instinctively feel is you. Hillman is suggesting that this uniqueness is our soul.

What's also interesting about the acorn myth is that the model of growth is one of *growing down* rather than *growing up*.

GROWING DOWN RATHER THAN UP

As Hillman says, *"The acorn myth is a worldwide myth that says that the roots of the soul are in the heavens, and the human grows downward into life. A little child enters the world as a stranger, and brings a special gift into the world. The task of life is to grow down into this world.*

"The perspective is that we came to earth as a stranger and slowly, as we mature, grow into the world, take part in its duties and pleasures, and become more involved and attached."

That is quite revolutionary for most people, and has massive implications. The acorn theory says that we—i.e. our core, our soul, the 'I' that is self-aware, the essence of who we are—selects the egg and the sperm.

That union results from our necessity—not the other way around. The myth says we choose our parents; they don't choose us!

In our experience at the Natural Gifts Society, adults often have a hard time grasping that concept.

But this is not the case with children. When we share this concept with children, they really respond to it. Children seem to just 'get' it.

One of the most effective ways to work with children to discover their Natural Gifts is through story telling. When working with children we usually bring a story such as *The Boy Who Dreamed of an Acorn* by Leigh Casler into the classroom to illustrate this concept. The story highlights the First Nations rite of passage for boys to find their gifts in the spirit quest.

It tells of three boys who must climb a mountain to seek dreams to guide them in their lives. One boy dreams of a bear; the second of an eagle; and the third—to his disappointment—dreams only of an acorn.

The meaning of the first two dreams soon becomes clear: one boy will become a great fisherman, the other a keen hunter. But the third boy must wait, watch an acorn grow into a tree, and strive to be as the tree, which gives freely to all. Only then is he happy and appreciated.

"...for the boy who had dreamed of an acorn became a man whose heart branched out wide like an oak tree, giving kindness and shelter to all who came his way."

Again, the children really 'get' it and respond to it.

When we go into children's classrooms, we bring an African or First Nations drum and wear some kind of decorative outfit, then we turn off the lights and transform the classroom into a nature scene.

We place a big candle in the center and when the children walk in, we invite them to sit around the candle in a circle. Their senses are immediately shifted out of the school environment and into, "Wow *there's a fire, and there's a strange looking guy with a drum ...*" and so their imagination is immediately piqued.

You can see pictures of these visits on our website, www.naturalgiftssociety.org.

The purpose is to help the children shift out of the box of culture and into nature, which in turn helps them to start wondering, "*What is my True Nature, and what are my Natural Gifts?*"

MEANING AND PURPOSE

> "*Life has no meaning. Each of us has meaning and we bring it to life. It is a waste to be asking the question when YOU are the answer.*"
>
> Joseph Campbell

To us, 'meaning' is an experience inside of us that is always evolving and always changing. By this definition, meaning is thus very subjective, and it is hard to pin down.

For example, what is meaningful to me may not be meaningful to you. And on top of that, what's meaningful for me today may not be as meaningful to me a year from now.

On the other hand, purpose comes out of meaning. In other words, once you discover what is meaningful to you, you would need to find a path, a direction, to utilize this meaning you've uncovered. The purpose is the goal of giving your gift to a meaningful need. When you live on purpose, you find more meaning in your life.

Remember our equation? $MAP = TN + EQ + NG - PR + MN$. In other words, one would experience more Meaning and Purpose (MAP) by first tapping into your True Nature (TN). From that place of True Nature (TN), you would receive your Essential Qualities (EQ), and then discover your Natural Gifts (NG). Next, you would have to remove any Personality Resistance (PR) that may block you from using your Natural Gifts ... and finally, you would need to find a Meaningful Need (MN) to apply that Gift to.

The best way to illustrate this concept is by giving an example. After tapping or resting into their True Nature, someone might discover that they have the Essential Quality of patience and a Natural Gift of teaching.

Upon discovering this Gift of teaching, a logical next step would be to ask, "Who specifically am I to teach?" In other words, they would look for a meaningful need to apply their gift of teaching towards.

However, there are bound to be Personality Resistances to stop them from applying their gift to this meaningful need. For example, the teacher may be terrified of speaking in public, or of being judged. These fears would be the Personality Resistance and the individual would require some help to overcome this PR in order for the Essential

Qualities (EQ) and Natural Gifts (NG) to be applied to their Meaningful Need (MN).

We have a friend who fits into this example beautifully; she was working as a teacher in a public elementary school. She liked her job, but felt unfulfilled at one point. She also felt blocked in her ability to fully express herself in public, and began to wonder if she should leave teaching in order to find a deeper calling that she was more passionate about.

When she told Dave, one of our authors, that she felt unfulfilled as a conventional teacher and was considering leaving, he suggested that she try 'bringing her soul to work'. She said she was afraid she would be judged.

Dave shared that he had been to a lecture with Eckhart Tolle, author of *The Power of Now* and *A New Earth – Awakening to Your Life's Purpose*. At the lecture, a teacher in the audience posed this same question, about whether to leave teaching or not. Eckhart Tolle advised the teacher that if he left teaching to pursue his soul, he might end up not finding it in the new situation. It would be better to take a risk and show up fully with his soul where he is now, in his present job.

If he were meant to be there, it would solve his dilemma. If he weren't meant to be there, then his current situation would spit him out of there and propel him towards his life purpose. If he didn't try, he would never know whether leaving teaching was the right decision for him or not.

Our friend took Dave's sharing to heart and decided to show up fully with her soul invested in her teaching. She bravely took a course to confront her fear of public speaking, and encouraged Dave to take it as well, so that he could also heal his own fear of public speaking.

Together, they both transformed their fear into the excitement of sharing their passion with others. Then she joined Dave's support group called *Living Your Purpose*. Over the next year she found the encouragement and support to integrate her new way of being into her teaching.

With healing and support she cleared these personality resistances and brought her soul fully to work. She is now one of the most passionate teachers we know, teaching children her passions—such as the mysteries of sacred geometry and the story of the universe, among others. She particularly loves working with children from ages eight to eleven because their imaginations are still wide open.

Her main passion, however, is helping these children to uncover their Natural Gifts. This is a very specific application, so if she doesn't match her Natural Gifts with the need in the world that is most meaningful to her, then those gifts are like acorns or seeds that aren't germinated.

But if she gives her gift of teaching to the very specific task of educating these children, then it is as if her acorn is taking root in the ground of being ... and it starts to become an oak tree, and produces many tiny acorns that all contain blueprints for other oak trees to grow.

It's an eternal principle, encapsulated in the one little seed. These children have been taught by a teacher who loves her work, and her students are going to remember this principle ... and the seed in them will blossom in the presence of someone who is standing fully in their own acorn, or their 'oak-tree-ness', of their own blossomed Natural Gifts.

She now recognizes and is surrounded by other passionate teachers who love their soul's vocation and are becoming mentors dedicated to bringing out the Natural Gifts of the children they teach. This is true education—from the Latin *educare*—which means 'to lead out' the particular gifts or genius of each child.

Instruction, on the other hand, is from the Latin *instructare*, which means to 'pack it in'—for example, to pack in information about acquiring skills.

Teaching through *educare* is a way that love expresses itself. It is, in fact, a deep form of love.

For example, in many of the European guild traditions, mentoring was a very important part of the culture, where masters would pass on the ways of their trade to their apprentices who had the unique gifts that resonated with the trade. This is a definite type of love, which our North American culture doesn't understand very well.

We believe that Meaning and Purpose comes out of experiencing our birthright; identifying exactly what our gifts are, and identifying to whom or to what we should give these gifts, in order to live with greater meaning and purpose.

Meaning and purpose is difficult to discover externally, as there are so many underlying agendas and cultural programming—from family, people, and events—that have shaped our lives. Most people are so conditioned that they spend years and often decades searching, and then give up because they are looking outside of themselves, rather than inside.

In this context, the analogy of the acorn with its hard exterior is very relevant. Breaking through that shell into the inside—in other words confronting your vulnerability—is very hard for most people to do. Sometimes, meaninglessness needs to be addressed or faced before the journey of transformation can begin. And that is a scary place to be.

In Eastern religions however, this is often interpreted as the act of surrender—which has nothing to do with giving up, and everything to do with having the courage to open yourself up to heal, receive and transform.

As we've stated, when we give our Natural Gifts to a Meaningful Need, we feel a sense of meaningful prosperity. This kind of prosperity needs to be both efficient and resilient.

Most businesses, for example, try to focus on *constant growth*. However, if we take a moment to look at this closer, we can see that Nature doesn't work like that.

Nature is seasonal; it ebbs and flows. There is a time for planting, being fallow, and harvesting. Thus, for meaningful prosperity, we need to look to natural cycles for guidance on what a sustainable life looks like.

GIVING YOUR GIFTS

As we mentioned earlier, our visionary members, Michael and Dave came together for what they described as *'a kind of saggy energy of meaninglessness'* seemed to be present in epidemic proportions in our culture and yet, many people in that same culture expressed a very real hunger to try to find the antidote to it.

There was an appetite for exploring such questions as, *"What's it all about?"* and *"Who am I?"* and *"What do I want?"* and *"What is my dharma?"* and *"What is my purpose?"*

Together with Michael and Dave, we soon realized that the first part of the whole equation was discovering that if you want meaning, you have to be *on purpose* with your gift. It's that simple.

Also, if you're not *giving* your gift, you can't have meaning—and so, how can you bring beauty into the world?

We realized there were two separate things we needed to be doing—one was helping with the Meaningful Design around the gifts, and the other was actually helping people to just 'rest' into those gifts, and get the support around that. Because, as E. E. Cummings wrote, "*To be nobody but yourself in a world which is doing its best day and night to make you like everybody else means to fight the hardest battle which any human being can fight and never stop fighting.*"

And so that has been somewhat our mantra in helping people get support around stepping into their gift and being who they are. If they are in their gift, they are in their genuine self.

Thus, the 'Why?' behind the Natural Gifts Society has been an attempt to create a foundation for people to be able to come and discover exactly what those gifts are. This brings them into alignment with their deep code of their life, their deep alignment with who they really are—which dials them into their original universal energy, where there is no real separation, just refinement.

The universal energy channels downward and it can be broken down into who we are in this body, with a piece of the universe running though our bodily systems, very accurately and deliberately, as a gift.

Who we really are is this gift from the universe, from the stars.

The ancient Greeks believed our destiny comes from the stars. And you can't just be any star, you can't live on any planet, you can't be any successful person you want—you can only be yourself, and share your own natural gifts. Wayne Gretzky couldn't be Michael Jordan, and Michael

Jordan couldn't be Wayne Gretzky. And who else could Pablo Picasso be but Pablo Picasso?

And so, that universal energy gets refined into who we are, and into our gifts, and when we step into those gifts, the *meaning* appears.

And as we deliver that meaning into the world, then beauty is downloaded into those areas of our life.

BLUEPRINT

When we started this work, we realized it was very much a passion for us. We wanted people to come back to their original selves, to their original agreement and their original code. We know that it is all a blueprint, and the gifts are like an acorn. That is why we chose to use the acorn as our metaphor, because an acorn is already a mighty oak that just needs to be sprouted.

We all realize that this is not just a little thing; it's a big deal. Also, we are interested in creating collectively, in resurrecting this idea of what Plato talked about, of having 'beauty schools' all around the world.

The members of the Natural Gifts Society are passionate folks who are tuned in to help connect people to their gifts, creating lives of meaning, so that there is more beauty in the world. Some of the greatest thinkers of all time, Plato and Socrates and Solzhenitsyn and Dostoevsky and figures from the Italian Renaissance and the Neo-Platonists all believed the same thing—that beauty will save the world.

And it will. It is exactly what we're talking about, and that's the 'Why?' of where it all came together.

We realized that we need to assist more people to live on purpose. It is going to come from each and every one of us, dialing into our own part.

Shakespeare said, "*Do your part, and therein lies the glory.*"

He wasn't talking about some Academy Award thing. He was talking about genuine delivery of beauty and intelligence, and who you are, and it comes streaming through you when you're in the thick of it.

CHAPTER 2:

TRUE NATURE ('TN')

We decided on the term 'True Nature' after studying spirituality and philosophy for many years. There are many other terms that people from all over the world use to describe It … the Source, God, Allah, Buddha, Self—some call it the *Ground of Being*.

We prefer describing *It* as our 'True Nature'.

Let's look again at our equation:

MAP = TN + EQ + NG − PR + MN

In order to have Meaning and Purpose in life, the first step is to tap or rest into the Source—into God, into the Universe, into your Self, into that place of infinite possibilities; your True Nature.

When you rest into your True Nature (TN), you will then discover the next step, your Essential Qualities (EQ). We will talk about Essential Qualities (EQ) later, but for now let's dive a little deeper into what our True Nature may look and feel like.

One of the problems we see in the world is that people have bought into the concept of separateness. Everyone is separate from one another, and so what's going on for 'them' doesn't concern me, and what's going on for me is separate from them.

However, consider this. When mankind put one of our own on the moon, we were able to look back at the earth from a distance. From that perspective, the view they saw was without any borders. They didn't see different countries; they didn't see different races, or different religions. All they could see was blue and green, naturally coexisting beautifully as one.

There is a story about the Apollo 14 astronaut Edgar Mitchell—while standing on the moon and looking back at Earth, he held his thumb up in front of his face, and the entire Earth disappeared behind his thumb. In that moment he had an epiphany.

The word *epiphany* is usually used in religious language, but in this case it was an astronaut, trained as an engineer and a scientist, who had an experience that he couldn't find words for. Mitchell looked all around, seeing the whole cosmos—from the Greek word *kosmos* meaning *well-*

ordered—and it felt like he was part of a Whole, and the Earth was but one small part of this Whole, and could be eliminated from view with just his thumb.

As he put his thumb aside, he was filled with an inner conviction that the beautiful blue green world of his birthplace was only one little part of an entire living system, harmonious and whole—and that we are all part of that whole, all interconnected in the Great Web. Later, he expressed it as '*a universe of consciousness.*'

This experience radically altered his worldview, and within two years of his Apollo flight, he founded the Institute of Noetic Sciences in California. 'Noetic' comes from the Greek word *nous*, which means *intuitive mind* or *inner knowing.* The Institute's primary programs are consciousness and healing, extended human capacities, and emerging worldviews.

We share a similar view that our True Nature is an infinite space of endless possibilities. Awareness is the essence of one's True Nature, so that one can tap into anything that speaks or calls out as a possibility. Within awareness the first subtle arisings are Essential Qualities (EQ) such as peace, love, compassion and so forth.

ANOTHER PERSPECTIVE OF THE MAP

There is another way to look at our equation—MAP = TN + EQ + NG − PR + MN—in a circular form. As you might recall from our meditation, we spoke about the limitations of language and our mission to try to go beyond those limitations where possible ... so here is the formula in an image format, with True Nature at the center. *(See diagram below)*

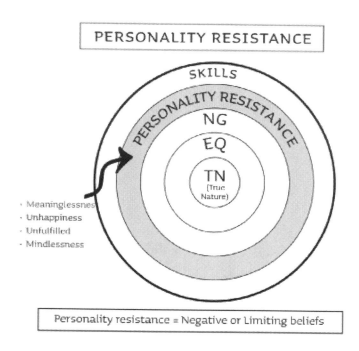

We use a compass as our metaphor, because the center of the compass needle is directionless, but not in a negative way; here it implies absolute freedom of choice. This illustrates that our True Nature is directionless. It's more of that *formlessness* idea. Our True Nature is actually inside and all around us.

Let's start outside the circle, moving in.

Skills are something that we can acquire. We can learn

to drill a hole. We can learn to use a word processing system. So, skills are really helpful tools.

But then we get to the Personality Resistance layer, and like the shell of the acorn, this can be an extremely hard layer to break through. People often find it difficult to go inside and discover some of the deeper, subtler levels inside themselves.

In this first diagram we can see the Personality Resistance is dense as represented by the darker color. When we are blocked on this level it is hard to access our inner resources or outer resources.

Just as we did in the meditation, we need to drop below, becoming aware of our Natural Gifts, right into the source of human experience, spaciousness that is formless. And then out of the formlessness come our Essential Qualities, which are really gifts from our True Nature.

If we go back to our example of the teacher, discovering her Natural Gift of teaching, she may choose to do the meditation, going into spaciousness, and then the Essential Quality of patience could arise.

We can all agree that the Essential Quality of Patience would be very helpful for a teacher to embody.

When we are aware that Essential Qualities are gifts from our True Nature for us, we can ask questions such as, *"What do I need today? Patience? Compassion? Peace?"*

Those Essential Qualities are available to us—if we just seek, then the solutions are usually right next to our problems. This sometimes occurs in nature—right next to the poisonous plant often grows the plant that is the antidote to the poison.

In the second diagram (below), we see the Personality Resistance cleared. The person can now access their inner resources and connect them to a Meaningful Need in the community.

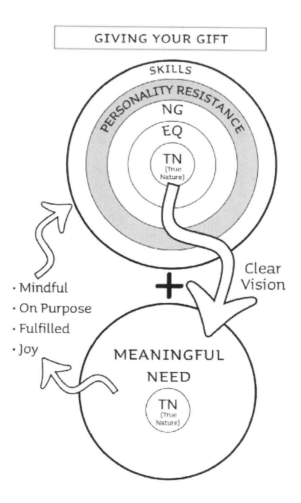

CHAPTER 3:

ESSENTIAL QUALITIES ('EQ')

*W*e have already established that our Essential Qualities arise out of our True Nature. These Essential Qualities are ways of being; patience, love, compassion, courage, forgiveness and so on. These ways of being allow us to excel in applying our Natural Gifts to the world.

Remember our teacher who was really blocked by a fear of public speaking? She had to dive deep within herself to discover the courage to confront this fear and to ask for help. Courage is an Essential Quality and comes from the Latin *cor* which means '*heart*'.

Our teacher had to find inner resources inside her heart to muster up the courage to change.

Edgar Mitchell too, had to discover inner courage to share his epiphany with the scientific community—risking his reputation with his peers.

On a daily basis, we need access to Essential Qualities such as love, kindness, peace, and so forth in order to survive and thrive. Some days we struggle, make mistakes, and need to look inside to find the courage, compassion and patience to forgive others and ourselves.

DAVE'S STORY

Whether you go to the moon, or the top of a mountain, or simply meditate, all roads lead to the ultimate reality; that place of True Nature.

The story of *The Boy Who Dreamed of an Acorn* taps into deep indigenous wisdom, but if you study traditions all over the world you will find that they all talk about different ways we can tap into something larger than ourselves.

Like astronaut Mitchell, one of our founding partners of the Natural Gifts Society also had an epiphany that transitioned him from a polarization between choosing science or spirituality, to embrace both science and spirituality.

Here is Dave's story:

"My father died of lung cancer when I was twenty-eight and the shock and grief were overwhelming. One of the ways I been taught to manage my grief was to keep busy and use substances to keep it repressed and to numb out.

"I had recently started an electrical and alarm systems company with a partner. He was an older man that became a mentor to me and helped me through the painful transition. We worked hard, and the company grew into a thriving business with thirteen employees. I had put all my eggs into the science basket, was a hard worker and was successful financially.

"After a few years I met and married a beautiful woman and was thrilled to begin co-parenting her five-year old son. Like many men I had been conditioned to repress my feelings, and so it wasn't surprising that I showed my love for my new family mostly by being a good provider.

"But eventually with the pressure of more responsibility I turned into a workaholic and did not attend to my health, my relationships, my friendships, my wife, or my step-son very well. Before long, they all started to suffer—especially my health—and yet by that stage, I felt so much responsibility for the company and to my staff, that I just worked harder and harder.

"Eventually my wife left me and took her son with her; it broke my heart when that happened. Again another wave of grief hit me that I couldn't cope with. My health was getting worse as well. I found myself asking, '*Why am I doing this? Why am I working so hard if I don't even have a family to go home to anymore? How can I justify this?*'

"After much agony, I sold my company ... and in my

mid-thirties, ended up having what is traditionally called a 'mid-life crisis'. All my identities were suddenly gone—father, husband, CEO, and journeyman technician—and when people asked, 'Who are you?' I could no longer say, 'Well, I'm CEO of this company. I'm a father, I'm a husband, and I'm a journeyman technician.'

"All of a sudden I was none of those. At that point, the burning question began: 'Who am I then?' If I'm not my personality, then who am I?"

"I basically crashed and burned. I was lost, confused, and was searching for answers. Some traditions call this major identity crisis *the dark night of the soul.*

It certainly felt like that to me.

PERSONALITY

"The word *personality* comes from the Greek word *persona*, which means *mask*. In the Greek theater, there were two masks, the comedy and the tragedy. The actors were clear that they were not the mask—they were the person peering through the mask. But today, we get so identified with how we act that we think, '*That's who I am!*'

"Of course, that's a false notion. In today's spirituality they talk about the false self, which is the ego/personality. Not that it's all bad—it has a certain role and function—but when we completely and exclusively identify with it, like I had done, we get out of balance.

"One of the first hints I came across was a quote from Einstein that said, '*The most beautiful thing we can experience is the mysterious. It is the source of all true art and science.*' That impressed me, because I was into science, and I respected the voice of a scientific expert.

"Up until then, I was not into religion or spirituality in the least. I had left Catholicism at age twelve, as there was so much emphasis on judgment that it produced a lot of guilt in me as a boy.

"And then I saw another quote by Einstein, which further oriented me towards the great mystery: '*A human being is a part of a whole, called by us universe; a part limited in time and space. He experiences himself, his thoughts and feelings as something separated from the rest—a kind of optical delusion of his consciousness. This delusion is a kind of prison for us, restricting us to our personal desires and to affection for a few persons nearest to us. Our task must be to free ourselves from this prison by widening our circle of compassion to embrace all living creatures and the whole of nature in its beauty ... All religions, arts, and sciences are branches of the same tree.*'

"Suddenly, it became very clear to me. And yet to my dismay, very few people around me seemed to understand this concept and experience. I realized that almost nobody around me really got the implications of what had happened with regard to Mitchell's epiphany or Einstein's profound insight.

"It was like everyone was caught in the matrix of separation and I had suddenly been given, like Neo in the film *The Matrix*, the choice between the red or blue pill.

"For a moment, I had a taste of a deeper truth.

"Things were not as they seemed!"

COMPETITIVE TRIBALISM

"All over the world today—people, countries, even religions—are still operating in a competitive kind of tribalism, fighting for survival. We haven't really integrated the fact that we're one living organism, called planet Earth or Gaia. And we're not all working together to address some very significant problems and concerns.

"We don't seem to understand that in order to survive, we all need to thrive on this planet.

"Scientists estimate that between 0.01 to 0.1 percent of all species are becoming extinct each year. They are warning us that we have to act *now* to change our habits, but we are so addicted to comfort that we go into denial and ignore them.

"It is helpful to contemplate when we humans will be the next endangered species.

"Instead, we're still operating on a mostly ego-centric basis, still believing that the person with the most toys wins. And that's causing a lot of imbalance in the world, a lot of haves and have-not's, and extreme polarizations.

"It seems as though the majority of humanity is stuck on a certain immature level of consciousness. Even in the wealthy countries, many people are really miserable in their work and in their life."

MY TURNING POINT

"Thanks to the insights I gained from Einstein and Mitchell, I started thinking differently, and seeing my role in the world through different eyes. As a result, some of my first moments of awakening came from watching films like *It's a Wonderful Life* or *A Christmas Carol* and realizing, '*I'm sleep walking, I'm not really awake in my life. I'm just putting in time.*'

"Looking back, I am incredibly grateful for those events that threw me into crisis. It's probably a cliché now, but the symbol in the Orient for *crisis* means both *danger* and *opportunity*.

"Usually before any real transformation occurs, there is a need to be honest with oneself, and a lot of inner work needs to be done. So in my mid-life crisis, I started smoking and drinking again—both alcohol and coffee. I had been using a triangle of coffee, cigarettes, and alcohol in order to keep myself in busy mode and to numb out the pain of not knowing who I really was and what my purpose was.

"Before long, my alcohol use got to be problematic and I had to admit that I had a drinking problem, just like my dad, and his dad, and perhaps many generations before that.

Fortunately, I met a good therapist and started making progress towards healing.

"One of the key turning points came in the fall of 1989 when I went to a talk by two men who were to become major mentors for me—James Hillman, the father of Archetypal Psychology and the author of *The Soul's Code*, and Michael Meade, the renowned storyteller, author, and scholar of mythology, anthropology, and psychology.

"That talk was a scary experience, as I remember walking down the hall towards the lecture room ... and there were about 200 men nervously lined up waiting to get in.

"At one point, I thought, '*Why is everyone so nervous? What am I getting myself into? Isn't this just a lecture?*'

"As the men entered the lecture hall one at a time, I could hear drumming sounds from inside. My nervousness increased and I began thinking, '*I'm getting the hell out of here!*' and almost turned around and left.

"However, the line kept moving and I inched closer and closer to the door. When people got really close, someone inside would open the door and shout, '*Go back. Go back!*' but then they would grab the next guy and pull him through into the gymnasium. It was bizarre! Before I knew it, it was my turn and they grabbed me and pulled me in.

"I was confronted by a group of guys chanting. There were drums and tribal masks from all over the world. They had symbolically created an ancient cave, with the African drumming, the masks and a simple, repetitive chant.

"The doorway of the gymnasium acted as a threshold that offered the choice: either you could stay outside—comfortable in your culture, the university environment, your conditioning—or you could come through into this 'ancient new world'. A symbolic death to the old world needed to occur in order to be brought into this other new world. Michael Meade calls this the 'world behind the world'.

"It was such a soulful moment, but at the time I didn't even know what the word soulful meant. Once I was pulled in, I suddenly heard a voice calling my name. A guy who had a company similar to mine was calling me and he was in the middle of this pack of about 200 guys. I went and sat beside him, and again I thought, 'Wow, *what the heck have I got myself into?*' However, we became good friends after that, and I became tremendously inspired by James Hillman with his concepts such as *The Soul's Code* and the acorn theory.

"Men were sharing on such a deep, honest level and it felt incredibly nourishing. One of the men invoked the grief in all of us when he shared about the recent death of his young daughter. This man would eventually become a very close friend and a co-founder for the vision of the Natural Gifts Society, Michael Talbot-Kelly. You will read about his story later.

"And then there was Michael Meade, sharing his potent African drumming and amazing knowledge of storytelling which he had collected from myths all over the world.

"One of the insights I gleaned was learning that

although most people think of the word *myth* as something nebulous—an untruth—in ancient traditions it pointed at something truer than true. Myths are big stories that point at some mystery that you can only experience. In this sense, world religions are great myths that point to great mysteries.

"And that's exactly what Meade and Hillman were doing that day—they were using poetry, mythology and drumming to share great wisdoms and mysteries, and this was a completely new world to me. I felt like I had been pulled into the heart of Africa or into the Celtic heart of Ireland, or into a more soulful masculinity and it stirred something inside me at the deepest level.

"Some of the poems that they shared came from a 13th century Persian poet and Sufi master called Jalâl al-Din Rumi—better known simply as Rumi. His poetry burnt a hole through my armor and I remember thinking, 'Wow, *this man really knows about love!*", not like the Hollywood kind of love that I've been raised on, or the confused love I experienced after my marriage broke down, when I truly didn't know what real love was and found myself in an existential dilemma.

"I like the word *existential* because this is at the root of my work as a Natural Gifts Mentor and Wholistic Psychotherapist today—to work with people whom I would say are suffering in an existential way. They are going through a major life transition like I was.

"In major life transitions the big questions emerge, which translates to, 'I don't know what my existence is about.' It generates questions like, 'Who am I? What is my purpose? What is meaningful for me?'

"I think that's the deepest kind of suffering, because you can't see the wound. It's not like when you've got a wound on your hand, a wound that is obvious and you can just get a Band-Aid and fix it.

"That is not so when you're suffering on an existential level. That's really deep suffering, and it can't be fixed with the attitude that one is broken. In fact, this kind of suffering can lead you to your soul's code and destiny."

ONE WORD FOR ALL SUFFERING

"I remember going to another talk much later by Michael Meade, where he shared that the United Nations had done a study of all the major countries in the world and the question they asked was: 'What's the greatest source of suffering in your country?'

"After a great deal of research and time spent, they had got it down to a list of four categories that described the most suffering in their country. Some of the words were things like 'rootless', 'powerless', 'futureless' and 'ruthless leaders', but then the authors of the study said, 'Now I want you to take all those words and summarize them into just one word. Distill those four categories into one single word that represents all the suffering in the world.'

"And the one word that they came up with was 'meaninglessness'.

"When I heard that, I realized that was exactly what I was suffering from. After losing everything—my house, my car, my marriage, my step-son, my business, my partner, my work—I was in a state of meaninglessness. It was like, 'What's the point?'

"Since I had sold my company for enough money so that I didn't need to work for a few years, at first I felt free. But eventually not having to work became a dilemma for me because I would normally have buried my pain with busyness.

"Instead, I went into a dark place that very few people can understand unless they have lived it themselves. This was indeed my dark night of the soul."

INDIA'S MONASTERIES

"In India, if you're unemployed, they've got a place for you. If you've got psychological problems, or you just want to loaf, or you just want to study spirituality, you can go from monastery to monastery to monastery, and they'll feed you, they'll give you shelter, and they'll give you meditation and books to read.

"The wisdom of India is that they know a small percentage of the population will not fit the status quo or will be in transition from one stage of life to another and they make a place for that. North America doesn't have a place for people like that—not in their organizational systems, and not in their belief systems. Mother India has a place for all her children.

"The result is that with the economic cutbacks of the past few years, we're putting people on the streets and we're labeling many of these people as mentally ill. Some of them certainly have got symptoms, but across the board these people as a whole are treated purely as objects ... undesirable objects, at that. No wonder they have symptoms!

"After I left the electrical business, I did a lot of inner work in order to heal and transform. For several years, I volunteered with seniors, which led to employment with them for seven years at a community center.

"It was appalling to see that our seniors were treated more like what Michael Meade call 'olders' than elders. There is rampant loneliness that happens when they get so isolated. They don't know what their True Nature is and what their Natural Gifts are.

ELDERS VS OLDERS

"In contrast to the medical model of viewing conditions that typically afflict our youth and our seniors like Attention Deficit Disorder (ADD) or Alzheimer's Disease (AD), Meade suggests that mythically when a society forgets their elders, the elders begin to forget their role in society.

"Mythically we can see Alzheimer's Disease or AD as

a kind of forgetting. In youth we now see Attention Deficit Disorder or ADD. Traditionally the elders gave the youth the right kind of attention in seeing and blessing their gifts, and they thrived as a result.

"Sadly, in today's world we are regressing as a culture, and going from ADD to AD!

"Consider that when a child isn't seen as carrying gifts, they might be labeled as having ADD and end up with a kind of label of AD in later life. Perhaps there is something 'right' in them 'acting out'.

"Again, if we think of humanity as one big family, most of our children lack the right kind of attention and thus are not seen as carrying gifts ... and our seniors are falling into forgetfulness of this role. One reason for this is that a large percentage of the people with means are middle aged and focused mostly on their own immediate wants and needs. We need elders who can see the big picture like in the First Nations practice of honouring the seven generations in all we do.

"Working with seniors and experiencing a kind of early temporary retirement helped me see that I was trapped in how I defined myself. I saw that many men felt lost when they finally reached retirement—myself included, even though it was on a temporary basis. I was caught in the painful ego comparison game, desperately trying to cling to some identity for fear of facing the fact that on an essential level, I was nothing. *No-thing.*

"I realized that I was neither special, nor was I less than ordinary ... I was an ordinary—yet unique—human being, just like everyone else.

"In my work with seniors, I would occasionally meet someone who was somewhat awakened, but most were entrenched in a lifetime of forgetting who they really were. I eventually realized that my time would be better spent helping people in midlife who were suffering with an identity crisis like I had been through. Hopefully they would not end up with the same fate as these seniors.

"This led me back to school to train as a Counselling Psychotherapist.

"Once I established a private practice, I noticed that many of my clients were in their midlife, ranging from ages 30-55. Sometimes they are referred to as Gen Xer's or the *lost generation*. These days, younger adults are also experiencing crisis and I am seeing them as clients more and more often. Many Millennials or Generation 'Y' born 1977 to 1994, are also suffering with what is popularly referred to as 'Quarter Life Crisis'.

"Again, it is an identity crisis that needs a deep awakening of their inner gifts and life purpose, as well as relational healing.

"Now many years later, I regularly practice resting in my True Nature. When I do this, Essential Qualities such as deep peace, compassion and patience often arise. My Natural Gifts are awakening and the impulse is to give them to others who are suffering like I was, for a greater sense of meaning and purpose.

"My mentors helped me to see that I was destined to experience suffering in my early life so that I could learn how to work through it for myself and with others. I'm not so trapped in the comparison and blame game, and I'm grateful for all of my past experiences—good and bad.

"For the past twelve years I have been joyfully co-facilitating retreats on discovering and expressing people's inner gifts. Once I learned that the Source of Love lived within me, and each one of us, I attracted a wonderful woman and remarried.

"I now enjoy a sense of calling, doing work that I love as a Mentor, Wholistic Psychotherapist and Midlife Awakening Specialist. I also feel much more like a balanced human being rather than a compulsive human doing.

"Working as a mentor and psychotherapist is very meaningful work, but at times I yearn to effect cultural change on a larger scale.

"Being part of stewarding the vision for the Natural Gifts Society is an attempt to address the existential suffering of meaninglessness on a much broader cultural level."

CHAPTER 4:

NATURAL GIFTS ('NG')

*N*atural Gifts are natural talents that we are born with. They differ from skills, which are acquired through learning and practice.

For example, someone can be born with the Natural Gift of wisdom. We have met children without much life experience, yet they are very wise. It can be really challenging for them because other people don't take them seriously until they reach a certain age. When asked how they know what they know, these children often say, *"I don't know, it just comes to me."*

Another example is someone being born with the Natural Gift of music. Learning and playing music just comes naturally to them. Of course, it is still helpful to practice if someone has the Natural Gift of music so they can evolve in their gift.

On the other hand, someone can learn to play music through study and practice, but it becomes merely a *skill*. There is usually a noticeable difference in the quality of music played by someone with the Gift, and these people experience great joy when they play for a meaningful need.

For example, a couple of musician friends of ours experience great joy whenever they play their music at seniors' homes and for people who are dying as they cross the threshold.

One of our founding members, Peter, has Natural Gifts such as entrepreneurial insight, leadership and wisdom. He feels a great sense of meaning and purpose when he gives these innate talents to a meaningful need such as the Natural Gifts Society.

He has recently started a group called 'Natural Gifts for Business' to help other entrepreneurs realize their Natural Gifts for living with greater meaning and purpose within their business life.

Sometimes our Natural Gifts are buried, and only surface later in life. Another one of our founding members, Anne Marie, has the Natural Gift of healing. It wasn't until later in life that she realized her gift of healing hands. Now she is a gifted Reiki Master, and Natural Vision Educator.

She also has the Natural Gift of administration, yet she often felt dissatisfied and unfulfilled when she performed administrative duties. However, when she applied that same gift to help the Natural Gifts Society, she felt great joy, meaning and purpose, and continues to give her gift by creating assessments and other programs for the NGS.

Our two visionaries and co-founders, Dave and Michael, had their Natural Gifts of Psychotherapeutic Healing, Encouragement and Facilitation awaken later in life after going through great personal losses. They found a vehicle for these innate gifts to come to fruition by training to become mentors and psychotherapists.

In essence, all Natural Gifts are healing gifts when given to a meaningful need.

THE GIFT ECONOMY

The principles of a perpetual cycle of reciprocity and inter-connectedness applies to Natural Gifts. Most indigenous cultures operate on what could be called a *gift economy*, or a *gift society*. For what we refer to as our True Nature, they often use the term *the Great Web*.

In fact, when it comes to indigenous cultures from all over the world, they originally didn't utilize a monetary system as we know it. The idea is that the Source, or Creator, created everything, including us.

They offer us the very wisdom that could point us toward a more sane and harmonious way to live sustainably with each other and nature.

Whenever we are being creative and giving our gifts, we are on purpose. To be on purpose, our task is to focus on giving our gifts in order to experience more meaning in our lives. In a healthy gift economy there's a cycle of Creator, Creativity and Creation—a circular trinity.

This enhances the Great Web of giving.

Each of us in the NGS has distinctive gifts to share, but we certainly don't have others. That is why we need the help of other people; people who have the gifts that we don't have. This fosters real interdependence and symbiosis.

YIN AND YANG

There's a movement enhanced by the ideas of an economist named Bernard Lietaer, who studies monetary systems and promotes the idea that communities can benefit from creating their own local or complementary currency.

Lietaer likes to call international currencies *Yang currencies* because they are so efficient. He refers to bartering and gift economies as *Yin* currencies, as opposed to the traditional *Yang* monetary systems. Such currencies circulate in parallel with international currencies.

Yin currency has the resiliency to build relationships and be sustainable. When everyone is giving their gifts, they love what they're doing, and they are giving what is unique to them. This fosters a healthy sense of community.

Engaging in yin currencies also offers a buffer if there is a major correction in the yang currencies as we have seen of late with the banking fiascos.

History has shown that local communities who have created their own monetary systems—systems that encourage resiliency and relationships—tend to not be so tragically impacted by the collapse of the major systems upon which everybody has become so dependent.

AN ALTERNATIVE TO THE YANG STYLE MONETARY SYSTEM

A young friend of ours has created a Yin currency for Vancouver, B.C. called *Seedstock*. It has different dominations and is legal tender. Here is how it works.

Seedstock comes into being when a local business commits to accepting Seedstock as at least partial payment for its goods and services. The business then gets to issue a certain amount of Seedstock and contribute most of it to a non-profit community group or project of its choice—maybe even yours!

The non-profit can then use the Seedstock to pay for salaries or rent or reward their volunteers. They may also use Seedstock to spend at restaurants that accept them. The restaurant can then use the Seedstock to purchase produce from a farmer who also takes Seedstock, or enlist the services of a participating accountant, and so on.

The downside is that—at least for the moment—they can only use it within a relatively small circle of people who are participating. On the upside, it is clear that this system is expandable.

"The planet does not need more successful people.
The planet desperately needs more peacemakers, healers,
restorers, storytellers and lovers of all kinds."

Dalai Lama

PART OF OUR MISSION

So, that's part of our mission in the Natural Gifts Society—to help correct imbalances and help to heal the meaninglessness—and connect people and nature with Natural Gifts, with our True Nature.

The more evolved teachings of spirituality and many of the spiritual traditions have a deep, mystical core that believes the spirit is within each of us and all around us. We are all intrinsically part of the creation, as is everything around us. And we are all One on an absolute level, yet unique on a relative level.

ANOTHER PERSONAL STORY

One of our founding members, Peter, shares his story of finding his gifts, and greater meaning and purpose within the Natural Gifts Society. Here it is in his own words:

"Okay, okay. Hmm. I don't know where to begin. I guess a good place to start would be the meditation at the beginning of the book. Whenever I do that, it draws my 'being-ness' into the present and helps me focus on what we want to accomplish.

"I find that ritual—and almost any ritual—to be a very powerful catalyst for bringing me into sharp focus. I strive to operate very much in the present moment. Moment-to-moment, all the time.

"And I am really aware that the things that come out of me are coming from the Source ... that I am purely a transitional vessel; a medium for higher thoughts to come through.

"That ritual helps me sift through all the stuff I'm thinking about, and all the messages and thought processes going on, but when I reflect about who I am and who my identity is, then I get confused.

"There's so much of my experience, of my contribution to the world, what I do and how it affects people, that seems to come from somewhere beyond me. It's hard to articulate, because it just kind of flows out.

"That's why I have a feeling that what we are creating—in our Society, and now in this book—is very powerful. The concept of what we have, and the relevancy of it, is so beneficial to the world, it's worth being passionate about.

"I see Natural Gifts happening all around me all the

time, and I agree with Dave's thoughts about linking us into nature, using nature as a reflection of our thought process, using nature in how we analyze or feel about our environment. It's just very natural. It makes sense.

"I see it all around us. I see it when I interact with people, during conversations. People talk about needing help, and I would use nature to address their needs, and reflect on it with them, and they'd say, *'Ah! That makes sense!'*

"I also love the story of how Dave arrived at his exploration of life and the Natural Gifts concept through personal crisis in his own life.

"And so I began thinking, *'What drew me to this concept? Was there an event, or a feeling inside, or something traumatic that happened? I had a million things I could have done with my life, so why choose Natural Gifts?'*

"For me, it was fairly logical. Like so many people that I've observed, I was very driven toward success in my career, working hard for security, working hard for my family, creating businesses, and chasing after money and material stuff.

"But always I felt a certain emptiness inside of me ... and this only got worse as I faced some personal challenges.

"I guess from an economic point of view, I was fairly successful. I graduated from university majoring in computer science, built a successful career in technology which grew rapidly and then I jumped to a higher level with my own company ... but then suddenly, I found myself in crisis—I was separated from my first marriage.

"It was a huge wake-up call; a time to stop and ask 'Who am I?' On a superficial level, I was the CEO of a company, an entrepreneur, with a lot of people that I felt responsible for, and I needed to take care of them. Problem was, I was not taking care of myself.

"And things just got worse. Soon after my divorce, my company went under mainly because of the impact of 9/11 and everything that followed, and I became totally lost.

"The days passed without any purpose or meaning. Sometimes I'd wake up, go to the mall and wander around aimlessly. I recall that on one occasion, my sister came with me to help me shop for shoes. When it came time to try on some shoes, I realized that I didn't even know my own shoe size! I couldn't remember that because when I was married, I had somebody else to take care of that kind of stuff for me. I had spent all my time and energy focusing on my work.

"It shocked me, the shoe experience. And so I began asking myself things like, 'What clothes do I like? What restaurants do I like? What kinds of food do I enjoy?'

"Most shocking of all, I had no answers!

"I totally had no memories of anything. It was like coming out of a prison, a decade in the dark, and coming out into the 'normal' world, the reality. It felt very strange.

"I realized I would have to re-create my own world, discover my own identity, discover my own meanings in life, and all of that. So I did a lot of self-searching, at the same time deal with a past full of bad memories, all the while trying to break away from that past life.

"That's when I went on a journey of personal growth, and discovered a lot about myself and did a lot of learning and experiencing."

WE NEED THE POWER OF OTHERS

"One of the things I discovered was that each of us has a different way of learning. For example, I've always been a strong thinker and very analytical. I am usually quick to grasp concepts and understand things on an intellectual level.

"But it's only when I actually experience something that I really get it. I discovered the power of *experiential* learning as opposed to university learning.

"One of the things I learned is that learning by myself is not enough. What's much more enlightening and enriching is meeting with other people, and sharing, and being vulnerable, and exchanging ideas, and getting validated. I discovered that learning by ourselves can lead to doubt, mainly because we only get one perspective.

"That definitely laid the foundation for my attraction to the principles of the Natural Gifts Society—the vision that we can come together to find and celebrate the natural gifts of society, and have a place to share that with others, to encourage that kind of thinking, to allow people to exchange ideas in that context.

"I think that's a wonderful way we each can use the learning, that we have experiences sometime in our life, and have a platform to exchange the insights we have gained. That is a great idea.

"I think the Society is also a wonderful forum for exploring our understanding of the universe and our place in it, and discussing things like separating scientific learning from the spiritual, non-scientific kind of learning.

"Things like perceptions of reality. Things like identity—how people have such a powerful association with their name, their career, their body, their material possessions and the external proof of their success. They associate success and wealth with money, and that's a kind of identity we need to take a careful look at.

"I'm fascinated that people often accept definitions and patterns of things as realities. For example, they look at the stars in the sky, and they see constellations. Each constellation is just a pattern of stars, and they give it a name, and that's a reality for them.

"But in fact, there is no constellation. There are just stars.

"Sound waves are the same. We hear music, or we hear someone say, 'Hello!', but in reality these are just patterns of sound waves.

"These things are really worth exploring, because in conversation with others we learn so much, and gain such valuable new perceptions and insights."

THE ROLE OF RELIGION

"Many people who are drawn to the Natural Gifts Society are artistic, philosophical, spiritual kinds of people, and when they find out that I come from the world of commerce and real estate, they often ask what brought me from that materialistic world into this world of self-awareness, spirituality, and self-growth.

"And I would say the simplest answer would be the search for greater meaning and purpose.

"I had been searching for ways to fill the hole that I experienced in my life; the emptiness. And so at first, I explored religions.

"I went to Christian churches, and Buddhist temples, and tried to find peace in that way. I found that a lot of the teachings were basically all good, and they were also all very similar.

"But one of the problems I encountered was that I found religions have a very strong opinion about what the 'right way' is. And if you didn't believe in their particular version of the 'right way', you are somehow doomed.

"That's one of the main reasons why I was attracted to the principles of the Natural Gifts Society—it was such a beautiful blend between science and religion, and not exclusive in any way. The Society, and the people in it, respected all opinions and are always open to exploring new ideas and insights.

"Don't get me wrong—I don't think religions are bad. I can see reasons why religions need to be opinionated, and to have strong guidelines and rituals. Not everyone operates in the same way, and one person may need that particular way to feel nurtured and secure on a spiritual and physical level.

"To me, however, the Natural Gifts Society, or indeed Nature herself, offers a mellow blend of spirituality, and a very good way of filling up the emptiness by embracing everything around us and feeling part of it ... of making peace with everyone and everything, and constantly exploring ways to explain the great mysteries."

"Your playing small does not serve the world. There is nothing enlightened about shrinking so that other people won't feel insecure around you. We are all meant to shine, as children do. And as we let our own light shine, we unconsciously give other people permission to do the same. As we are liberated from our own fear, our presence automatically liberates others."

Marianne Williamson

CHAPTER 5:

PERSONALITY RESISTANCE ('PR')

ANOTHER ACORN ANALOGY

We compared the personality earlier as the parts of us that are like masks in the Greek theater of the comedy or tragedy. Each of the masks of our personality is like the roles we identify with.

Some typical roles are: the responsible one, the controlling one, the victim, the critic, the perfectionist, the pusher, the parent, the pleaser, the hero, the rebel, and so forth. Our ego is the central role in our personality that we identify with at any given moment.

Freud called our ego the *executive function* of our

psyche. For example, if a person identifies with the part of them that always needs control, then their ego is said to be controlling.

When we undergo a major change in identity, our ego feels threatened by the impending change and will create personality resistance. This is normal, and in some cases healthy. Our ego is just trying to protect us.

If many of our identities fall away, like it does during a quarter life crisis or midlife crisis, we would experience an identity crisis and feel a sense of meaninglessness until a new direction emerges.

Dave's story is very relevant to the context of this book and the scope of the Natural Gifts Society, because this meaninglessness is so pervasive in our modern world. It could perhaps be the core problem that the Natural Gifts Society is trying to address in our work and by writing this book.

The personality resistance Dave described is like the acorn's shell—it's hard and it protects what's inside. And what's inside is vulnerability. When we delve deeper inside, there lies the blueprint for the eventual oak tree.

But this vulnerability can also be very scary. In order for the acorn to become the mighty oak tree, it first needs to root itself into the ground. Only from there can it grow toward its natural potential and true fulfillment.

The meditation we began with is part of the cure to meaninglessness. If you go past the misery, the scary parts, and past the shell of the acorn—past our personality structure—and you honour the senses, the body, and the breath, and go even deeper, you eventually reach the heart of the acorn, what some traditions call the soul.

From there, you discover your unique blueprint of gifts.

What some people fear about meditation is that if you go deeper, there is a danger of becoming nothing. And the ego is terrified of that.

In Buddhist meditation, they talk about going into the nothingness. But when you actually experience it, it is really 'no-thingness'—you experience the pure generative nature of the universe and you tap into your fundamental source of creativity.

However, most people identify with their ego so they are very afraid to try anything else. That is why Dave had to go through the initiation in the gymnasium with Hillman and Meade; to get to a deeper way of being. It can be scary to enter the unknown.

Unfortunately, most modern cultures don't help their adolescents to be initiated into mature adulthood, unlike many aboriginal cultures, who do have well defined initiation and rites-of-passage ceremonies near puberty, which help them discover their unique reason for existing and meaning and purpose.

Tribal culture explores such fundamentals as "Why was I born?" "Who am I?", and try to determine their very specific purpose.

In essence, it's fundamentally about finding meaning and purpose in our lives.

GETTING PAST THE EGO

*"You can search throughout the entire universe
for someone who is more deserving of your love
and affection than you are yourself,
and that person is not to be found anywhere.
You yourself, as much as anybody in the entire
universe, deserve your love and affections."*

Buddha

Another reason why we began this book with the meditation was to illustrate how strong the ego is in all of us. In the Western culture, we are conditioned to think thoughts such as *I am breathing*, as if I am in control of my breathing.

You might recall how we suggested changing the perspective so that you feel the Universe breathing in and out of you. In a way, by doing this we're fooling the ego in order to circumvent it. We honour the ego/personality, but transcend and then include it.

In a recent television interview, Dave discussed a methodology he was trained in called Voice Dialogue, in which he talks to different parts of a person's personality. He spoke of the shift in perspective that results from the insight of becoming aware of 'the Universe breathing in and out of you'. The interviewer was intrigued, and asked him if he could demonstrate it to her.

He took her through the meditative exercise, and soon she was following his lead and saying, "I *am breathing in, I am breathing out. I am breathing in, I am breathing out.*" He pointed out that although that was true from the perspective of her relative ego-centric personality (that is, it was a relative truth), the greater truth was that instead of seeing herself as breathing in, she could let go of control and experience that the *Universe* was actually breathing into her. Now that's an absolute truth!

One sign that shows we are evolving, by the way, is the ability to hold more than one perspective with awareness.

Each moment of our lives, the universe is breathing out into all of us, into the plants, into the animals, and then when we breathe out, the universe is breathing in. That's an absolute truth—and so right away, a radical shift in perspective from the *separate me* to a *Great We* occurs.

In that simple moment, you become part of the Oneness.

At the end of the interview, the cameraman commented, "*....when you led that meditation, I completely went out into the universe and I totally forgot what I was doing, and when I came back I thought, 'Wow, where was I?'*"

It is so powerful when we do this because we shift our

identity from the ego to expanded awareness. Because the ego personality is on the horizontal plane, it works in opposites—parent and child, right and wrong, good and bad, thinking and feeling.

So in our normal thinking mode, the personality stays on that level, and our perspective is two-dimensional, and remains on that level.

In order to transform our perspective and bypass the ego, however, we have to introduce a vertical plane, like a cross:

At the top of the vertical plane is *Awareness*. All meditation traditions around the world basically want to experience a 'witness place' where you can objectively observe yourself. The simplest word for that is awareness.

If you followed the suggestion we gave in our earlier meditation, you may have reached a moment where you realized, "*Okay, the ego thinks I am breathing.*"

That's good—but it's still a limited perspective. As soon as we contemplate what we are perceiving or experiencing, that is what we call a relative truth. But the absolute truth—which is a greater truth—comes from the unlimited Self, and that's the realization that the same breath is breathing us all. Most people can experience that pretty quickly.

Now, some people have a false notion—they try to live in the awareness. However, if you think of awareness as being like the spotlight that illuminates the stage of your life, then one part of us wants to be in control, and the other part of us can release and surrender. We all have both of these parts of us. And these are functions of a normal healthy ego/personality.

But what we were doing in the meditation was saying that if you want to go beyond control then you're going to have to relax and just surrender into *being breathed*. And that's the equivalent of resting into your True Nature, into the Ground of Being, into the Oneness.

By just allowing yourself to be breathed, you become part of everything. You're part of the plant, part of the planet, and part of the entire universe.

You're in that place that Einstein referred to; where you know that it's an optical delusion of your consciousness to think you're only individual and separate.

In reality, you're like a unique cell in the body of this entire universe.

Earth has this little envelope of air around it and us, and all throughout history everyone has breathed the same air that we're breathing right now. It may be more polluted now, but essentially it is the same atmosphere.

And so, here is a new perspective—by breathing and becoming conscious, you not only connect with all the people and plants and animals in the world today; you also connect with the essence of everybody and every living thing that's ever been.

And to bring that idea to another level, think about

a plant that is producing oxygen—we need oxygen to survive, so it's helping us to survive.

And each time we exhale, we breathe out carbon dioxide, and that in turn helps the plant to survive.

THEOLOGY, PSYCHOLOGY AND SPIRITUALITY

The journey that Peter took—from materialism to spirituality via religion—is quite common with regard to several Natural Gifts Society members. And so, we'd like to explore a little more about some of these aspects.

The term *psychology* comes from the Greek word, *psyche*, which means *soul*.

Working as a Wholistic Psychotherapist, Dave noticed that many of his clients were struggling with the religious training of their childhood.

Since Christianity is such a predominant religion in North America, he took some courses towards a master's degree in spiritual direction at a school of theology to see what the current perspective was. There were several Christian denominations represented at this university, and they mostly agreed to disagree when there were differences. Sometimes they would even get into very heavy discussions and intense arguments.

What troubled Dave was that they focused too much on their *differences*, instead of *celebrating their similarities*.

This seemed to reflect the dark shadow of religious tribalism, and he found it difficult to accept the ostracism of someone wearing a turban or dressing in orange robes, or because their name for God was different from someone else's.

CARL JUNG'S INFLUENCE

Renowned psychologist Carl Jung was not a theologian, but his story is highly relevant—as is his contribution to the world of spirituality, psychology and philosophy.

The story goes that Jung had many male relatives including his father, who were all pastors or theologians. And so it would seem he had little choice but to also become a pastor or a theologian.

His partially autobiographic book, *Memories, Dreams, Reflections* tells how he had powerful dreams that spoke to him. Jung also saw that his father, when he got really sick, really didn't believe in God. He would talk the talk, but when it came down to it, he didn't really have the faith. So Jung, as a boy, was thinking, "*Well... do you really believe, or don't you?*"

Around the time when he went to the Christian ritual of confirmation, he was excited to think that he would finally have a revelation or some big, divine experience. Unfortunately, it was a non-experience for him.

And so, Jung started studying all the different traditions around the world, and being a complex thinker,

81   CR

he tried to integrate everything, as did Joseph Campbell, whose writings on comparative religion and comparative mythology are extremely valuable for anyone interested in the concepts we have been talking about.

The bottom line is that Jung came up with the concept of the collective unconscious, which does not develop individually, but is inherited.

The collective unconscious is a universal point of reference, and he believed that every human being is endowed with this psychic archetype-layer at birth. In other words, it is not something we can acquire by education or any other conscious effort, because it is innate.

Some people also describe the collective unconscious as a 'universal library of human knowledge', and see it as a kind of muse or sage; the transcendental wisdom that guides mankind. Jung taught us how to dialogue with our Unconscious through active imagination.

Jung believed that the religious experience must be linked with the experience of the archetypes of the collective unconscious. Thus, your god-image is lived like a psychic experience of the path that leads you to the realization of your psychic wholeness.

In essence, he described how to work with our own transcendent function and follow the path of our unique destiny and gifts, the path of individuation. When an interviewer once asked Jung if he believed in God, Jung said, "*I don't need to believe, I know!*" Jung's destiny was to answer the call to experience the Truth or Gnosis, beyond mere believing to direct knowing.

Referring back to *The Soul's Code* author James Hillman, he eventually branched off from Jung and founded what became known as Archetypal Psychology.

This was opposed to the popular developmental psychology movement at the time, which suggested that our character structure totally determines who and what we will become.

Archetypal Psychology, on the other hand, taps into the similarity seen in many indigenous traditions. There's something innate within us that is connected to a Higher Power, whether you call it God or Allah, the Universe, or, as we call it, our True Nature. This innate soul's code is like a unique image deep in our psyche that we can relate to for ongoing meaning and purpose.

The problem with language however is that all words are 'form'. And the trouble with form is that it doesn't include the formless. That is, it doesn't include the mystery.

We love the word 'mystery', because if you define it too closely, it's no longer a mystery. That's why in our meditation we spoke of listening to the sounds, and then listening to the silence.

If we are to journey deeper into the soul, we must be willing to journey inward and be surprised.

As St. John of the Cross taught, "*God only said one*

word. *And that word, God uttered in the silence.*"

And so this teaching points us inwards. Rumi would say, "*Stop all the words now. You've got to go in, you've got to experience the truth for yourselves.*"

DREAM WORK

As psychotherapists, Dave and Michael tend to work with people's dreams a lot. It's one of the most powerful methods, because you can't make up your dreams, and they can really introduce you to the Subtle or Soul Level of consciousness.

Dave facilitated a series of psychotherapy sessions for a gifted teacher who suffered terribly from migraine headaches. She had tried everything medically to get rid of her headaches and had no luck.

Since she couldn't get rid of the symptoms, Dave invited her to explore her symptoms with awareness. Paradoxically, when something like a painful symptom is happening 'to' us and we try everything to get rid of it, we feel powerless against it when it doesn't change. We usually don't consider making it worse.

In some cases, this is unwise. In this case, Dave's client felt stuck and safe enough to explore it. As they slowly invited the migraine to unfold in her experience it suddenly changed channels from the physical channel to the visual channel in the form of a dream. All of a sudden she remembered her reccurring dream of her mother criticizing her.

The memory of the dream was still painful but not as painful as the migraine headache she had been experiencing only moments earlier. As Dave facilitated her experience within the dream, two characters stood out; one representing her as a victim daughter, and the other representing her critical mother as persecutor.

In her early family history her mother had indeed been very critical of her, but now one part of her personality had become an internalized critic that took the image of her mother in the dream

Once she integrated the message from her dream, she realized that she had disowned her Essential Qualities of power and discernment—represented by the inner critical mother. She eventually embraced her power and discernment and learned to be more assertive. Then she was able to set healthier boundaries in her relationships that had previously turned abusive.

Her personality resistance was blocking her ability to fully give her gifts in her work with people. Integrating the message from her symptom and dream helped her to be more assertive and to establish healthier boundaries with others while still maintaining connection with them.

After completing a series of sessions with Dave, her migraines were so significantly reduced that she could return to her love of teaching and continue to give her gifts. Whenever her migraines returned, she knew she was getting out of balance and just needed to rebalance.

LEVELS OF CONSCIOUSNESS

A simple way to talk about levels of consciousness is to consider that right now, as you read this book, you are awake in the normal sense that we use that word. It would be hard to read if you were asleep!

But there are levels of wakefulness, or consciousness. When we first go to sleep at night, we're no longer awake and we enter a dream state. So that's a different level of consciousness. And then when we go into deep sleep, that's a different level of consciousness again.

This is all pretty normal—everybody experiences it. Every day, almost everyone goes through these three levels of consciousness at least. And they don't usually think about it.

In spirituality, the first level is called the Gross Level. The Gross Level is being awake, but we're operating mostly from our ego in this moment.

The next level is the Dream State, which is equivalent to the Subtle Realm. Even in a waking state you might get a little hint of this, like you might see an owl or something fly across the screen of your mind. In fact, we're actually dreaming all the time. Our symptoms are our body's way of processing dreams.

Let's expand our understanding of this by referring to the Vedic belief that human experience passes through three states—Waking, Dream and Deep-sleep.

In the Waking state, there is the experience of the solid external world through sense perception.

In the Dream state, our senses do not function. The impressions left in the mind by previous experiences are brought to life and shaped into the likeness of waking itself. The internal perception by the mind of these revived impressions lodged within—as if they were realities of the waking state itself—is the Dream.

In deep sleep, neither the senses nor the mind function. The self withdraws into itself as it were, but there is no self-understanding. The self is covered by a primeval intelligence from which springs all waking and dreams.

It depends what tradition you're trying to follow, and for now, here's a simple analogy of the Gross Level:

If we look at a simple wooden chair, and we touch it, it feels solid. We could say it is on the gross level. But if we examine it with an electron microscope, we would see right away that it is made up of the finest particles with lots of space around them.

In fact, there is both a particle and a wave.

And even when you try to separate the particle and the wave, you'll find that one moment the wave is a wave and then it can flip and become a particle, and the particle can flip and become a wave!

So the very smallest microorganism or micro-particle, or whatever you want to call it, of this chair, turns out to be not solid at all.

If we apply that learning to language, we see that nothing is finite; language can in fact be very inexact—one teacher prefers to call words signposts. When we apply meaning to language, we find that all language is 'gross' in a sense that it's pointing at an experience. Of course, some language is more precise than others at pointing toward what we are inferring.

While reading or experiencing the meditation earlier, you might have touched on it.

When we started, we were in our normal ego personality level, thinking, *"Okay, I'm going to meditate."*

Well, maybe part of you thought, *"No, I actually want to get busy and do stuff... you know, I've got a lot to do today."* But at that point you probably decided, *"Okay, I probably need to surrender to this for a while, or if in a group, the others will think I'm rude or unenlightened or something."*

And then as we went inside, you might have started to experience more subtle experiences, such as your senses. That's still at what we are calling the Gross level. Then, as we continued to move inside, you might have started to experience a deeper level, maybe a feeling of peace. That's encountering the Subtle level.

And so as you start to become aware of being deep inside, all of a sudden you might think, *"Hey... I was pretty* agitated when I started this, but as I've gone inside I'm feeling a whole lot better."

The peace is inside.

And if you go beyond the peace, then you get to the Unitive Realm, which is spacious awareness and Formless Intelligence.

CUTTING THROUGH LANGUAGE

From what we've learned, the human realm is constantly changing and evolving, but it's all held in something that doesn't change. In Christian mysticism it's called the Godhead, and you see the same thing in Hinduism where Brahma is the Formless.

But then it emerges into the Trinity as three levels of consciousness, three different forms that the Trinity can take. In Hinduism it is called Brahma, Vishnu and Shiva.

Same thing with Christianity—there's the Godhead, 'that which can't be named', but then it emerges as Father, Son, and Holy Spirit. Using language with True Nature in mind, a possible nature context is Creator, Creation and Creativity.

And so we can get creative with language, but there's a problem if language stays only in language and people end up fighting about the differences—the semantics of their language—and they start fighting each other over a different name for what is essentially just a signpost.

After all, water is water, whether it is called *aqua*, *eau*, *vesi*, *voda* or *das Wasser*.

What we're hoping to do with the Natural Gifts Society is to go beyond all the dogma, beyond the language, right to the essence. As an analogy, think of installing an alarm system in your home or business. It can be very complicated and technical, but the customer isn't interested in all the technical details.

In fact, if a system is too complicated, they won't use it. They want something really simple, like a red light for stop or 'off', and a green light for go or 'on'.

It is the same with psychology and spirituality. If you get down to the essence, it's actually really simple. Your True Nature, Essential Qualities and Natural Gifts are the essence of you.

MIND, BRAIN, SOUL AND CONSCIOUSNESS

Dr. Daniel Siegel is one of the leading cutting-edge figures in the science of interpersonal neurobiology. Together with people like Dr. Norman Doidge, Paul Bach-y-Rita and Jon Kabat-Zinn, he has helped to advance the understanding of the human brain in quantum leaps.

Amongst other things he explores how to apply the interpersonal neurobiology approach to developing a healthy mind, an integrated brain, and empathic relationships. Another of his findings is that our minds are partly defined by their intersections with other minds.

Said another way, we are wired to 'sync' with others, and the more we sync (the more psycho-emotionally we connect), the less our brains acknowledge self-other distinctions.

During one of his talks we attended, he said something like, "*I can't really talk about the soul from a science perspective, but there's something there that's a mystery that we can't quantify yet.*"

Here is another brilliant therapist, transforming important understandings of psychology and spirituality by acknowledging that there is expanded awareness and a soul perspective!

Dr. Siegel then said, "*We didn't even have a definition of the mind! We didn't have a coherent definition of emotions until recently.*"

He told a story of how he was at a conference with about forty experts in their fields—anthropologists, psychologists, biologists, and the like, and he asked, "*Do we have a definition of the mind?*"

The answer was "*No.*"

There was no definition of the mind that anybody could agree on at least. Or even the brain! And it's been virtually omitted from our teaching and training at universities.

So, towards the end of that day, Dr. Siegel went for a walk, and when he came back he had a new definition of the mind: *"The mind can be defined as an emergent, self-organizing process that arises from, and also regulates energy and information flow within the brain and within the relationships with others."*

When he presented this definition to the conference, all forty of the professionals said, *"I can buy that."* They could buy into it, because they could each find a way in.

And the mind, according to his definition, isn't just located in our bodies; it's an interpersonal relationship.

And it's a field of consciousness. We are connected to each other and to everything in Nature!

Another exciting development in integrating spirituality and science is the introduction of brain science in some schools. For example, they teach the concept of mindfulness and also a simple hand model of the brain, the latter developed by Dr Daniel Siegel .

You begin by holding up your hand with fingers outstretched, and fold your thumb in so that it touches your palm.

Then fold the top four fingers down over the thumb. This now represents our brain, with our eyes at the bottom of our hand, the top of the head above the knuckles, and the wrist being where the brain stem starts, connecting your body to your brain.

The palm area represents the brain's stem—this is like

the reptilian brain. It's the oldest part of human evolution, and it still operates very much like a cold-blooded animal; like a crocodile, or a serpent. It's also where we find the fight, flight or freeze mechanism—our instinctual response to defend ourselves.

The thumb represents the mammalian brain, or the amygdala, and this is our human warning system.

Where you have curled your fingers down, the fingers represent the cortex, which is the most recent development of our brain, and the bottom parts (where the fingernails are) represent the prefrontal lobes.

Dr. Norman Doidge, Canadian psychiatrist and author of *The Brain That Changes Itself* wrote that our brains have neuroplasticity, that they can be rewired and changed.

It's wonderful news for psychotherapy, for people who thought they had traumas and labels that they could never change, and it's really good news for spirituality too, because we know that through meditation we are actually bringing about physical changes in our brain.

Finally, scientific proof that meditation works!

But of course, many of us didn't need science to tell us that.

It is now understood that when you engage in mindful practice, you can actually build new neural networks in your brain.

And so, in the same way as Dr. Siegel came up with a

definition of the mind that people could agree on, at the Natural Gifts Society we believe we can use Nature—as in Natural Gifts—to relate to everybody what meaning and purpose is essentially about.

.

CHAPTER 6:

MEANINGFUL NEED (MN)

"But history will judge you, and as the years pass, you will ultimately judge yourself, in the extent to which you have used your gifts and talents to lighten and enrich the lives of your fellow men (women). In your hands lies the future of your world and the fulfillment of the best qualities of your own spirit."

Robert F. Kennedy

MANY PATHS

The meaningful need you give your gifts to, is subjective for each person. For example, you can have four people with the Natural Gift of compassion but their meaningful need can be completely different.

Let's say the first person may give their gift of compassion by feeding people without enough to eat. This is what is meaningful to them.

The second person may give their gift of compassion through hospice work, attending to those who are in their last moments of life.

The third person may share their gift of compassion through volunteering at a Veterinarian Clinic, helping with cats.

The fourth may volunteer in a wildlife shelter, working with wounded birds.

However each person decides to give their gift, each will feel greater joy, fulfillment, meaning and purpose when their Natural Gifts are given to whatever is precisely meaningful to them.

The key is that when there is a match, it will feel natural! When we give our Natural Gifts creatively to a meaningful need, there is often a feeling of being in alignment with the Creator and Creation. We feel as if we are going with the flow.

Often synchronicity occurs in the form of coincidences or what Jung called meaningful chance. The more we are grateful for our gifts, it seems, the more meaningful chance happens. We start to feel blessed.

There are two wonderful contemplative thoughts from Sufi master Hazrat Inayat Khan which sum up the deep connection with nature:

"Nature is the one sacred manuscript by which all the others have been inspired.

"To the eye of the seer every leaf of the tree is a page of the holy book that contains divine revelation, and he or she is inspired every moment of his or her life by constantly reading and understanding the holy script of nature."

You don't need to be a priest or a rabbi in order to have a sacred life. Your work can be your temple, your offering. And this is what we're doing with the Natural Gifts Society— we're bringing deep democracy to spirituality.

We're saying, it's not just an exclusive realm of mainstream religions, but rather it's an innate thing, a 'religious instinct' as Jung called it.

This innate instinct, he believed, is true of all human beings. So then, we believe it comes back to the individual person. Each person is unique.

The same Sufi teacher we referred to before said, *"There are as many paths to the Beloved, as there are human breaths."*

Most people actually have a hard time with so much freedom. They'll all dress the same way, or speak the same way, but often find it hard to acknowledge that they are free to choose.

Especially today, they have access to the Internet— and that means they've got access to the whole world and all its teachings. They have the freedom to study whatever calls to them.

A post-modern Buddhist teacher, Ed Bastian, created the Spiritual Paths Institute which honours most of the world's wisdom traditions.

Bastian has come up with an innovative way to honour each person's unique learning style when considering what spiritual path is best for each individual. It looks like he is catching the wave to the InterSpiritual future.

What's important is to go inside and find out what's true in there. That's what the Buddha said. *"Don't believe me. Go inside. Find out for yourself."* That's why contemporary forms of Buddhism appeal so much to the scientific community, because it's really objective, and frowns on too much dogma belonging to another time, place and culture.

There is much research being done on the efficacy of meditation and mindfulness. Science is beginning to prove that meditation is beneficial.

The Dalai Lama appreciates scientific inquiry as well as spiritual practice, he sums up his essential spiritual view when he says, *"My religion is compassion and kindness."*

INTEGRAL SPIRITUALITY

We were talking about different levels of Christianity, and different kinds of spirituality, and that topic wouldn't be complete without introducing some ideas from one of the Western world's leading contemporary philosophers and writers, Ken Wilber.

Having noticed that when post modernity came along, many people threw out a great deal of the benefits of religion in order to move towards science. Wilber thus took on a noble undertaking.

He believed that a lot of religion had become what he called *mythic*, in that much of it was superstition and there were many elements that belonged to a certain cultural period and time.

In addition, there were some real prejudices—for example, against women and the LGBT (lesbian, gay, bi and trans-sexual) community.

The trouble is, as Wilber saw it, post modernists threw the baby out with the bathwater.

Thus Ken Wilber's life work has been about creating an integral approach, like Joseph Campbell did with mythology.

How do we bring the science to spirituality and get the essence of both of them, and let go of that which doesn't serve us anymore?

He calls it *integral spirituality*. He is a prolific writer with a comprehensive body of work including such classics as *Integral Spirituality*, and *A Theory of Everything*.

His work is profound; there are several universities now offering master's degrees in integral studies. The integral perspective is spreading and now there is integral medicine, integral education, integral spirituality, and integral psychology.

Wilber's Integral theory expands our understanding of perspectives with his articulation of the four quadrants of human experience. He speaks of the four perspectives as 'I, We, It and Its.'

If you imagine a box with four quadrants (*see diagram below*), the upper left quadrant signifies the interior subjective or 'I' perspective.

INTEGRAL SPIRITUALITY

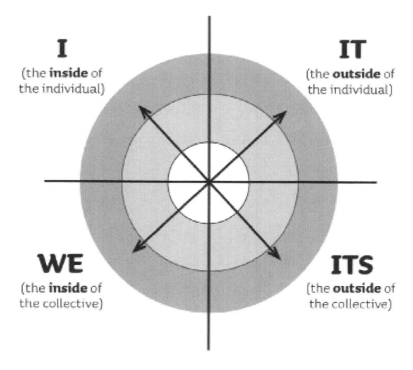

Source: The Integral Operating System by Ken Wilber, 2005

The interior portion of our map TN+EQ+NG-PR refers to this upper left domain. This is where our inner world of psychology and spirituality reside.

Then the upper right corner is the singular objective perspective of our cells, organs and body. Objective Science resides here.

The lower left in his model is the 'We' of relationships. Finally, the lower right is the 'Its' of cultural systems, for example, organizations, and countries.

Our Meaningful Need (MN) resides in either of the lower quadrants or both.

For integrated development it is important to have healthy psychology, spirituality, bodies, relationships, organizational structures and groups.

When we discover our natural gifts, it is important to keep our body healthy and to give our gifts to transform our self, our relationships and our society.

ACCESSING DIFFERENT PARTS OF THE SELF

Our personality layer is really useful at times, but when it takes control of our entire life, then that part of us that wants to control everybody and everything is not going to release and let us get to some of our inner resources.

One of the methods that we use is to honour the part of us that controls us, and interview it. This can be done individually, with a partner or in a group.

At times we all naturally move into the part of us that gives us control, for example when we drive our car. At other times we need to relax, but the 'controlling part' won't let go.

It is helpful to have a practice of working consciously with this part of ourselves. A method called Voice Dialogue is skillful at this. By relating to this subjective part with some objectivity, it can transform.

We move over and identify with this part and notice how we feel, perhaps feeling serious and tense. We allow this part to express itself without judgment and then move back to the center and relate to it. We acknowledge it and ask it, *"What's your role?"*

The answer usually is, *"My role is to take control."*

We ask: *"And if you had your way, what would you do?"*

Often it responds with, *"I would control everybody and everything. That's my job, to take control."*

And we say, *"Well, if that's the case, I'd like your permission to talk to another part of the personality, and I would like you to control any other parts of the personality that try to interfere with the self that I ask to speak to please?"*

When it gives permission, we return to a center position.

Next, we ask to speak to the part that releases, the part of you that can just relax. Then we move over and rest into relaxation.

By acknowledging it, the part of us that takes control,

we learn to honour it and work with it. In this way, we harness our personality to give us access to deeper aspects of our spirituality.

But if you try to get to meditation before you acknowledge the ego, then the ego will often resist it. And this is why a lot of people get stuck for years, sometimes decades, trying to meditate.

They're trying to use a purely spiritual approach, when knowing a little bit about psychology can help them to honour their ego and the role it plays, and then actually get its permission to go beyond the ego, to get to their inner resources.

Also, when you complete your meditation, you actually can bring, say, the patience and the peace to the ego, and then apply those essential qualities to your daily life.

With practice, this becomes easier and easier to do. In fact, you can meditate anytime, anywhere, and it doesn't have to take a long time.

Let's take an example of driving your car to work. Inevitably, you're sometimes going to find yourself caught in a traffic jam. That's when your patience is really tested to the limit—especially if you're in a hurry to get somewhere— and it's quite natural for that impatient, intolerant part of you to emerge.

You might start swearing at a driver who has just squeezed into the queue ahead of you. At this time it's useful to acknowledge that a part of you is angry.

Just acknowledging that *it is only a part of you* gives you a little space to access the resource of your awareness. Then you have some choice, instead of being totally hijacked by your emotions.

Try to observe yourself. Your thinking might be something like, *"That guy's an idiot!"*

Then you might think, *"I'm sitting here swearing, grabbing the steering wheel with white knuckles, and the guy I'm swearing at doesn't even hear me! He doesn't even know I exist!"*

When you realize the absurdity of that, you might tune in and notice that underneath the anger there is some fear of getting hurt by his driving.

You can start taking some deep breaths and consciously acknowledge that part of you that goes into defense on your behalf, trying to protect you by keeping you in control. It is normal to feel scared when there is chaotic driving that could endanger your health.

Then, relaxing into intention, move deeper into those places where you might find patience, understanding and compassion. Perhaps begin with forgiveness, and say, *"I forgive myself for being impatient, a part of me felt scared."* This is showing compassion to your self.

Then, *"Let's imagine that guy is swerving in line because he's frantic. He's just got a call that his wife is in hospital having a baby ... or maybe his mother is dying. And he's on his way to the hospital to see her one last time."*

Even if this is not his reality, perhaps you decide to send him some compassion for whatever is stressing him. This, in turn, causes you to feel better.

When we practice this over time, we find it is easier to forgive someone by considering a compassionate reason why they might be doing what they are doing; something we don't like and have a reaction to. And suddenly, we find that our anger is gone, the anxiety's gone, the tension is gone—and we feel a whole lot better about everything.

BLENDING SPIRITUALITY & SCIENCE

Dave tells an interesting story of an insight gained during his spiritual journey:

"Eventually I was committed to a spiritual path, and was initiated into the Sufi tradition. I started to wear clothes of that culture, I eventually became a center coordinator, I had a spiritual name, I was teaching classes, and I even taught a series on living your purpose. There are some wonderful teachings on that topic in that particular tradition.

"Before long I was starting to feel like, wow, people are getting to know me as this spiritual guy—and soon, it became a full-on spiritual identity. It felt really good, because people projected the image of a spiritual teacher onto me, or some kind of superior being, or at very least a perfect guy. My spiritual ego was getting pretty pumped up!

"But then I would come home, and my wife would say

something as innocent as, *'Let's clean the house!'* I would start to feel annoyed. One minute I was feeling high, then the next I was getting moody. Over time I began to see that I was using spirituality to bypass the ordinary aspects of my life.

"Needless to say, that popped my ego bubble, and a big shift happened at that point. I learned that I needed to work with my psychology and my spirituality to be an integrated person. Now I see myself as being on more of an integrative, wholistic or psycho-spiritual path.

"I remember one teacher teaching that *'the spiritual rubber meets the road in relationships'*. Of course there are many mature Sufi teachers and students who also work diligently with their psychological limitations, but I was immaturely getting trapped in spiritual inflation.

It is a great paradox that we are human and somehow divine!

And so, these days I want to integrate both science and spirituality. I want to integrate my humanness. I'm just as frail as any other human being. For example I recently had the flu, and man, I was out of commission. If I don't sleep for a few days, I'm a wreck.

"I've realized that I'm just as ordinary as any other human being ... yet I also realize that there is something unique in each one of us.

"I also believe it is important to acknowledge that some people are more evolved than others, because they are standing in and delivering their Natural Gifts.

"There is a need to honour our ego personality—the one that drives the car, the one that likes to have some control—because its job is to keep us safe and deliver our gifts.

"The Sufis taught me that every human being has an essential seed of the soul, something Sufi master Hazrat Inayat Khan of that tradition called the 'God Seed'. The God Seed is that unique aspect of the divinity within each person.

"Jews call the God Seed the *Divine Spark*. Christians call it *Spiritual Gifts*, or your *charism*. Think of those with charisma: It's when they give their charism, their Spiritual Gift, that they become charismatic.

"There is a monastery, St. Catherine of Siena, that specializes in assessing and teaching about Spiritual Gifts. This is one of the places where we drew inspiration from in developing the Natural Gifts."

UNDERSTANDING OUR EMOTIONAL REACTIONS

When we think back to our experiences in the traffic jams, this is all highly relevant. At some deep primal level, when we see something that annoys us—such as a driver sneaking into the front of a queue—we temporarily 'flip our lid' as Dr. Dan Siegel calls it.

Or, imagine that you're having an argument with your partner, and suddenly you flip your lid. Your ability to reason and talk things out goes offline.

At that primal level, you feel like your smoke detector is sounding, and there's a fire, and you need to do something fast.

To our limbic system there's a savage tiger that's been let loose, and your life is in danger.

Your emotions and thoughts can send you into panic and then into reaction. Instinctively, we feel a powerful urge to either go into fight or flight.

That may be the best strategy if there was indeed a fire or a tiger, but it's probably not the greatest strategy in relationships—unless you are facing someone with a serious intent to harm you.

Often what we are facing in relationships is a disapproving look or tone of voice, but it seems like a tiger to our defense system.

Thus, a better strategy would be to learn *how to calm down your alarm system.* Once you know how your system is wired to protect you from danger, you can learn to more accurately assess the situation and send a message to your brain to say. "OK, *brain, I'm just fine and keep breathing, I'm actually safe here."*

By doing this, gradually you will calm down, inviting into your experience calmness, compassion and forgiveness, three essential qualities from the Source.

Can you see that by just using your imagination to consider, *"Hey, what if this guy is on his way to the hospital because his wife's having a baby?"* you can actually consciously invoke your inner resources to calm and soothe your brain?

BRAIN IN THE GUT

Our brain is not just the grey matter in our head; it's our whole nervous system.

In fact, experts now say we have a kind of 'second brain' in our heart, and a kind of 'third brain' in our gut, an extensive network of neurons lining our heart and gut that is filled with important neurotransmitters, which in connection with the brain in our skulls partly determines our mental state and plays key roles in the body's innate intelligence.

So, next time you notice that your heart isn't engaged in the decision you want to make with your head or you get a gut feeling about something, perhaps you'll take it more seriously!

By using insights from neuroscience, and simple imagery, and easily understandable examples, we can speak the right language and make sense of some fairly complex processes.

We need to ask people, *"What language do you need to hear that works for you, so you can get the benefit of this?"*

Yes, we want to bring in Nature, because Nature is so often left out, and without Nature, we're all in trouble. We are earth (our body), comprised of water (seventy percent), fire, air, and minerals in our bones … we are Nature.

And yet people will say, "*I'm going to go out somewhere into Nature*" which is an oxymoron and a separation, because we *are* already 'nature'. It's our egoist identification that causes the separation. It's also interesting to note that the word 'sin', etymologically, means 'separation'.

Another way you can interpret sin is from the Aramaic word for sin, meaning 'missing the mark'. It's as if you were aiming for the target of remembering your True Nature, but you just missed the mark! And that's a sin in that sense.

The term 'original sin' is really grossly misunderstood in much of Christianity, and many people, some Catholics in particular, say they often felt guilty. As one woman put it, "*I had to even go into confessional to prove that I was guilty! As a girl growing up I often couldn't even think of why I was guilty, so in the confessional I would just make up sins. I would lie, because I didn't know what else to say!*"

How confusing is that? As Peter said earlier, without doubt, there is a place for religion to teach moral behavior to large groups of people. But the shaming that happens, and the guilt, often requires that people need to do some 'de-programming'.

Mystically, the term 'original sin' means that we are each an individual unique manifestation of the divine.

When we forget that, we are in separation and missing the mark.

Abraham Maslow, the father of humanistic psychology and creator of the well-known 'Maslow's Hierarchy of Needs', suggested 'self-actualization' and 'spiritual values' are at the top of his pyramid and are some of humanity's great needs.

He had an interesting thing to say about religion. He said all religions—Buddhism, Christianity, Islam and so forth—were all started by mystics, people who had the experience of the Mystery.

People were attracted to these mystics, such as Christ, or Buddha, and some of them experienced the Mystery as well, although many others didn't—usually because they didn't have the consciousness to be able to understand and integrate the teachings.

Some of these people formed groups and then organizations, and before long, these people got qualifications, even though they hadn't had the direct experience. This is how you end up with a limited form of Christianity, for instance, that's sometimes far removed from the teachings of Jesus.

The Bible teaches about Jesus kicking the moneychangers out of the temple, saying to render unto Caesar what is Caesar's and render unto God what is God's, and that you can't serve two masters—you can't serve money and God.

Jungian Psychotherapist Dr. James Hollis said in a recent lecture, *"You can see the discrepancy in our architecture—you look at any city in the world, and you look downtown, and instantly it tells the story. The churches used to be the highest buildings, now it is the financial institutions."*

Think about it—in any small town or village, anywhere in the world, the highest building was the mosque, the church, or the temple, pointing toward humanity's highest values. Now, in our modern cities, it's the bank towers, the insurance towers, corporations, and super corporations.

So, money is clearly the new god of the ego. And we have to really be clear about that. Money is a very useful tool, as long as we don't make it our master.

We believe that one of the reasons why so many people are suffering today is because our culture teaches that money is what we should all be striving for, and if we primarily go after money and success, then we'll be okay.

Undoubtedly, that is serving the wrong master.

PART 2

CHAPTER 7:

MEANING AND PROSPERITY ('MAP')

MYTH OF ER FROM THE SOUL'S CODE

In Hillman's own words:

"It is a worldwide myth in which each person comes into the world with something to do and to be. The myth says we enter the world with a calling. Plato, in his Myth of Er, called this our paradeigma, meaning a basic form that encompasses our entire destinies. This accompanying image shadowing our lives is our bearer of fate and fortune.

"The acorn theory expresses that unique something that we carry into the world, that is particular to us, which is connected to our 'daimon', a word rarely used in our culture."

Another meaning of 'daimon' is your particular genius, your 'genie in the bottle' inside of you. The myth of Er is the same in all cultures around the world, and everybody has a particular contract to deliver their genius, their gifts.

In the first half of this book, we spoke of coming into the world with a distinct code, with something to deliver. In order to wake that code, one often needs a teacher or a mentor. Sunshine is also needed on the sprout in order for that 'acorn' to send its roots down and grow up into an oak tree.

The sun needs to pass over it so that it cracks. And in the heat of that cracking, the sprout goes down and then starts to come up. And then, through those ordeals of coming up and becoming larger and larger, the mighty oak shows up.

The second half of this book is to look at the Natural Gifts Society's vision, and how that is manifesting itself. We will work through the analogy of the Transformation process, from crawling caterpillar through to becoming a butterfly.

Our grand vision is to have several Natural Gifts schools or centers around the world, with a hub of Natural Gifts Society (NGS) 'elders' who help co-ordinate and act as mentors. We envision having these places where people can be assessed, to bring forth who they really are, and be shown the technology, the art and science of becoming that in the world.

A lot of people are symptomatic, meaning that they are not in alignment with their gifts. They may have become lost in the everyday shuffle of life and now need to find their true source.

As poet John Keats said, *"It's a business of soul-making"*. The whole universe is conspiring to get us doing exactly what we know to be true inside of us. And when we dial into it, the world starts to reflect that.

THE NGS ANSWERING THE CALL

Some young people today carry huge burdens—the possible end of the world, loss of diverse species, burdens such as losing our indigenous cultures through mindless development.

Our young people see the good, the bad, and the ugly. A common choice for them is to veer towards apathy: *"I'm just going to get annihilated here anyway, so what can I do? I can't do anything anyways, so why bother? I might as well just get annihilated by drugs."*

One of our favorite lines from Bohemian-Austrian poet Rainer Maria Rilke, says: *"The task is to constantly be defeated by greater and greater things."*

Thus, if we can positively influence even one person,

if just one person hears an authentic conversation such as, "*I see who you really are. I see why you're suffering, and I'm part of the problem. I acknowledge that my generation and our current lifestyle have squandered a lot of the world's resources. And I don't really know what to do, but can we talk real with each other? I've suffered too. You know, I turned to alcohol when I was in pain,*" then all of our work has been worthwhile.

We know that suffering transformed into meaning can bring enlightenment and can actually bring about progress. *Man's Search for Meaning* by Viktor Frankl tells the story of how he ended up in a Jewish concentration camp, but even in the most tragic, horrific conditions, Frankl found meaning there.

Indeed, we can be part of the solution instead of part of the problem. The challenge is to become less isolated, and band together with those with a common mindset and a common goal.

When there is support, life becomes much easier.

Other age groups besides our youth need support and direction as well—these include the elderly who have lost their purpose, and those struggling with mid-life questions.

One of the most common issues we encounter is a loss of identity. So many people reach a point in mid-life where they find they have spent a great deal of time and energy on building a career and chasing after success and material things, and they increasingly start hearing questions like *"Is this what it's all about? Why am I doing this? Are my sacrifices worth it?"*

If you are in your gift, and you know your gift, and you're performing your gift, and you know that those receiving your gift represent a meaningful need, then you will have little doubt.

It is also about creating balance. So many people have an identity crisis and find they are attached to all the wrong things. They may have over-identified with a career image, or have become stuck in a pattern of addiction or obsession.

Joseph Campbell expressed it well, describing it as *'a larger life'*. You're in the service of something larger—the whole universe, if you want to go that far!

When you are serving a meaningful need, it's a beautiful thing to behold. If you've got the gift of healing, for example, you could go into the area of medicine and surgery and know that you are connecting your gift with a need, and that is your purpose, and when that comes together, there is nothing but joy and beauty running through the system.

In essence, we are all supposed to be living a specific life. It's not a random life; it's an accurate life. There is exact wisdom and knowledge.

We have been taught to think we can be whatever we want to be in life, and while that may sound like a wonderful freedom, it is fraught with problems. We need to come back to what is absolutely fundamental in the territory of our being, and that is to accept that we have particular inner gifts, gifts that we are meant to be sharing with the world, serving a meaningful need.

WOUND TO WOMB

It is painful to be wounded ... but there's a possibility for the wound to become meaningful. If you work that wound enough; it can eventually become a womb. And out of that womb comes new life: possibly a new you.

(*'Rekhem', the Hebrew word for 'uterus', comes from the same root as the word 'rakhamim', meaning 'compassion'. And so the word 'compassion' shares the same root as 'womb'.*)

We've seen it over and over again. People come in with the worst suffering, but once they shift their perspective on it and see some of it as a blessing, as a guideline towards what needs to be learned, it can become a powerful basis for recovery and rebirth.

Sometimes it will take a great deal of patience, and a lot of compassion—especially towards yourself. But you emerge so much stronger.

That's why we find the image of a butterfly emerging from the pupa, from the mush of a caterpillar, so powerful. We will speak more on the butterfly as a symbol later.

GROWING AND COMMUNICATING

NGS is a new organization, and so we accept there may be some challenges ahead. We will be developing more ways to support and bring people aboard, and writing this book is only one small step towards this.

It's said that ninety percent of any conflict is not in the content, but tone. It depends who is speaking and how they are saying it. On the flip side of that, if we want people to hear our language and message—truly, deeply hear it—we need to understand that ninety percent of real deep hearing, compassion and healing has to do with us embodying the message.

To have others embody this work and take it in deeply, we need to speak from a deep place of authenticity.

We think that authenticity is ultimately the essence of it.

CHAPTER 8:

THE CATERPILLAR STAGE

Continuing our theme of telling personal stories from some of the founders of the Natural Gifts Society, we believe these stories are important to others because they invariably incorporate issues that we hear time and time again from new people we meet.

Here is another story from Peter about overcoming adversity, about coming to terms with issues in his youth that he tried to suppress for many years, and about how his life has changed since he found his true self.

Symbolically, his wounds are turning into a womb that births new life. He is transforming from a caterpillar to a butterfly as he gives his gifts to a meaningful need for meaningful prosperity.

Let's hear him tell his story:

"I have a bunch of stories about growing up, and feel like I had a very tragic life and childhood.

"For a long time, I felt immense shame when I talked about those early years. But now, years later, I am actually proud of my roots, and I believe my background is quite relevant to this book and ironically, are the very reasons I decided to devote my time to the Natural Gifts Society."

TREASURE MAPS

"There is a new self-assessment tool called 'treasure maps', where you are encouraged to go back as far as you can remember about yourself growing up. For example, you might start at the age of five, and write down the names of all the people you can remember from that time, people who were important to you and had an influence on you. Then you might jump to age ten, and do the same, and then age fifteen, twenty, or whatever.

You write it all down—'mind map' it all—you jot down everything relevant that you can recall, any incident or event that left an impression on you. The exercise is all about finding out who you are, how you got here, and why you are the way you are today.

I come from a wealthy Chinese family living in Vietnam; however, as a result of the intense political crisis in that country, we fled to Hong Kong as refugees. We were what was known as 'boat people', crammed into whatever would float ... sometimes two hundred people in boats designed to hold fifty.

"We sailed from China to Hong Kong, and lived in refugee camps for a while before coming to Canada. It was a very dark time for us, and very difficult. My whole family was very well educated but the only jobs we could get were really low end ones—thankless work for minimal wages.

"Not surprisingly, during my early years in Canada I didn't feel at all comfortable with myself. I felt I was underprivileged, and was always looking around at other people and thinking how better off and lucky everybody else was.

"This plagued me throughout my youth and teen years, through university, and well into my adult life. I was very self-conscious, and pretended to be somebody that I was not.

"In retrospect, I appreciate all the things that happened to me. In fact, it's a story I am actually proud to share because it's a wonderful example of how we can overcome adversity and become whoever we want to be.

"Much of my growth since then can be attributed to working with the Natural Gifts Society and finding my true self. One of my biggest epiphanies, for example, was realizing that who I am - who I truly am, is not a result of what had happened to me in my childhood years.

"I gained the self-confidence to know that life is more than the reality that most people project, and that the past and the future are unimportant—all that really matters is the present moment, for that is where reality is.

"And that is where we have all the power to make changes in our life—in the present moment. And when that particular present moment passes, we will be in the next present moment, and so on, and so on.

"I also realized that it's not just about having the awareness, but being able to recognize it, to see it. Nature's gifts are all around us; we just don't see them because we are mostly not aware of them.

"What I see this Society doing is to illuminate this awareness in people. That's one of our most important objectives.

"A second objective is to develop a community to support this illumination and make it even brighter."

CATERPILLAR TO BUTTERFLY

Peter's story represents a recurring theme that we encounter—how people go through tough times and traumatic experiences, but are able to turn those wounds into a womb for rebirthing a new you.

It's really like a caterpillar turning into a beautiful butterfly, and taking flight in a new world.

In deep psychology the butterfly is the symbol of the soul. We have the opportunity to transform from the egocentric caterpillar into the soulful butterfly.

As one of our colleagues says, at a certain point you can look back and see that you were 'in training' all along. You have to go through these ordeals, these initiations. *Wound to womb.* The initiation from caterpillar to butterfly. This is the soulful language that we now have come to understand and find meaning in.

These ordeals were spontaneous, a time when the golden threads of your destiny became the entanglements of all those wounds. But eventually you own it, you claim it, and you can look back and see that the 'training' was essential to get us to where we are today.

We believe in honouring that. Without the caterpillar dying and turning to mush as a pupa and undergoing metamorphosis in its protective cocoon, there can be no butterfly, no soul.

Another common theme is that one of the purposes of life is to be present. But really, how present are we? Our entire past acts like a filter, so we are all carrying our history with us, and through that filter we can only perceive so much of the present reality.

This is why part of the work we do is initiatory work, to help them come to terms with past issues from a new perspective. We help them by taking them back to what happened in their formative years, to understand their journey and bring them to the threshold of initiation, when they are ready.

THE NGS VISION: ANOTHER PERSPECTIVE

There was an African elder who taught Dave and Michael that when you are born into that culture, the shaman interviews the fetus to find out what his or her purpose is.

It turned out that in that particular tradition, we would both be members of the 'mineral clan', and it has become our vocation—it's our true calling.

The task of the mineral clan is to help people remember what their gifts and purpose is. This is from one of the oldest cultures on the planet ... 50,000 years of uninterrupted culture, and they're still doing the same thing!

Best of all, we learned that if you can't listen to your purpose at the beginning, if you can't hear what's going on in the womb, or at birth, you can pick it up later. And that's what we realized there.

And so, our personal mission has been the mission of our friendship, and we extended it into an organization because we realized that as individuals we couldn't do very much. As a group of friends together, we can do a little more.

Our message is that the main suffering in the world is from a lack of meaning, and the antidote is to find your true nature, your soul's purpose, your gifts.

Indigenous peoples' traditions of helping initiate youth into meaningfulness, to find their unique purpose, and to be on track with that purpose allowed them to evolve into mature adults.

We envision growing what we call 'Natural Gifts Circles', where a few friends come together as a circle, sharing and displaying their gifts, appreciating gifts, and learning how to take their gift and give it to the meaningful needs of others.

As Picasso said, *"The meaning of life is to find your gift. The purpose of life is to give it away."*

Following the purpose of those gifts is exactly what it's all about.

INITIATION AND RE-INITIATION

In many indigenous cultures, one initiation isn't enough. Sometimes you are given a new name and you go through an initiation every seven years.

We find that astounding—every seven years you get a new name, so that you don't identify with the previous age, the previous period in your life, the history and the baggage associated with that stage.

It's also interesting that biologically, every seven years we basically become a new person. Through natural cell regeneration, we have an entire new body every seven years. We don't have a single cell that's older than that.

The wounds that we all carry are what qualifies us, and that's why we believe we can speak with authority and depth on this matter. We have gone into the wound enough that we find meaning in it.

But unfortunately this thinking is still pretty revolutionary for most people, and there is still a certain degree of shame around talking about these things. In general culture you will often get ridiculed.

We are hoping that as we get our message out to the masses, people will become more comfortable with these ideas, but we also believe that the best place to start is to grow our Society from a base of people who really want to listen to our message.

Part of the eldership is to be able to see those tears as gifts. There is nothing more 'authentic-making' than tears. But if those tears are seen by somebody who doesn't understand and doesn't have true compassion, they will tell you to 'keep a stiff upper lip', or say things like, 'big boys don't cry', or you will get shamed for acting like a sissy. And so, one of the important things is to provide that 'eldership gaze'. This is the gaze of blessing that sees who we really are.

When a butterfly first comes out of its cocoon, the wings are kind of stuck together, for days sometimes, and if the wind and sunlight doesn't get to them, they don't dry and the butterfly won't be able to fly away, and it will die.

So, just as the butterfly's wings need that drying period, which requires the 'gaze of the sun', so too, we need the 'eldership gaze' from our mentors to strengthen us through the initiation process.

The soul's code is all about being seen, and you need those mentorship moments as we call it—you need somebody to be able to see you being transformed. You need someone to see that your wound is actually a womb.

You need someone to observe that and say, "*He or she is transfigured, but we need to hold our gaze on him or her, we need to hold the warmth.*"

The Dalai Lama and his doctor talked about the warmth that is missing in our culture, and the warmth is what comes back when we are 'on gift' and we are with our brothers and our sisters and we are connected in the community and in the village.

One of the sad and frustrating experiences of those of us who have tried a lot of things to get initiated, such as going to African tribal elders, doing workshops, sweat lodges, and more, is that after we have experienced those initiatory moments and we go home to Thanksgiving or whatever else, other people see you as if you were still the same person they knew before.

In traditional culture, your parents would have been initiated, and almost everyone in the village would have been initiated, and your siblings and friends would all be familiar with the process and hold it in the highest respect.

And so, after you have been initiated, your parents would no longer address you as their child—because now you are an adult. Similarly, your siblings and friends and neighbours and family would also see you as this new person, and treat you as such.

This is one of the problems we are facing. In our modern society, there is no coherent village, and no coherent community, and so our youth are trying to self-initiate with drugs, high speed car chases, diving off cliffs, and so on.

As Eckhart Tolle says, mountain climbing, cliff diving and such is evidence of trying to live the intensity externally and to avoid that incredible gift of what you can discover inside.

And so, it's all externalized like the caterpillar, constantly consuming until it exceeds its own body weight. In the cocoon it starts to dissolve the old caterpillar identity. Then new cells emerge that become imaginal cells and eventually a butterfly.

Even some organizations and countries are like that—they are like big caterpillars, constantly consuming—in fact, it's called a consumer culture. And so the entire country will have to go through a transformation of consciousness to get those 'wings' to be able to go to the vertical flight for awareness and perspective, then come back and land again for soulful living.

To continue the analogy, the caterpillar is constantly consuming, so it's outwardly referenced, but the butterfly on the other hand is about *pollination*. The butterfly is spreading the nectar of the flowers around to create more pollination and beauty.

The analogy is that if we can transform our consciousness, then we will be spreading beauty in the world. We will no longer have a whole culture of people who are always externally referenced and consuming finite resources. We will have people who respect the inter-relatedness of all things and who can spread the beauty of their gifts all around.

Therefore, not only do individuals have to transform, but companies also have to transform, and even entire countries have to transform in order to get to the pollination of working together as a species to bring the gift of more beauty into the world.

MICHAEL'S STORY

Earlier, we read about the journey of two of the founding members at NGS, Dave and Peter, and how they had walked through the fire to become who they are today.

We also discussed the concept of transmuting a wound into a womb, so that we can be reborn—reborn into the life, the dream that we are meant to be living.

We also shared how giving our gifts lead us to a life of meaning and purpose. This giving fosters greater meaningful prosperity.

The next story is told by another one of our founding

members. We think you'll find it equally impactful and relevant.

Here is Michael's story:

"Well, I think at some level I was born in an African village. That's been my problem all my life, because that's where I had a fully functioning village around me—a thriving family, the ancient Irish culture and nature herself in all of her glory—when I came into this world. I was seen, blessed and witnessed in all of what I'm all about in this lifetime right at the beginning of my life.

"Why has that been my problem? Everything since then has fallen short of this standard, this quality of blessing, of 'Village-ness'.

"Seriously—when I was born I received that deep embrace, that deep hug at the door into this world. I had that home that we are all searching for. I was born in Ireland into an old farmhouse. Everything was laid out. I had culture intact, I had nature intact, I had my family intact. I had three brothers and three sisters to play with. My family was financially well to do, creative and very popular.

"And then one spring at the age of 10, we came to Canada. And instead of the type of welcoming ceremony that I was used to, what I experienced was exactly the opposite. I somehow knew on the drive in from the airport that this experience was not going to go well.

"There was no intact culture or nature, as we moved

into a row house in a grey spring of downtown Toronto. My mom and dad split up shortly after, my dad lost the job he was promised and had a nervous breakdown, there was very little money to go around, where there was plenty before.

"Then I was raped, beaten up, and witnessed brutal regular gang violence and a murder.

"That was the start of the deep initiatory shock of loss and separation in my life. I was brought to the lip of insanity.

"By the time I was thirteen, I somehow recognized that as bad off as I was, there were people around me who were in worse situations. Sure, there were lots of people living in mansions in downtown Toronto and in the rich suburbs, but there was suffering in these homes as well busy and absent parents, addictions, kids wanting to spend all their time with our family and not be in these big empty houses they lived in.

"We were in a reasonable lower middle class suburb, but there were also the poor areas—areas where I witnessed lots of street people, mental health and addiction issues, violation and oppression of every kind.

"So I realized that I needed to start helping. Because as bad as my situation was, if I stayed with that wound, I knew I would go nuts. I literally felt like there was a line I was going to cross.

"By helping people, two things I knew for sure: one,

I got some relief from my own suffering. And the second thing was, there was this voice that I heard inside my head that said, *"You're going to write a book entitled 'Stories for My Grandchildren' that will result from helping others and from being of service."*

"I didn't understand it back then, but I somehow knew that I would have to collect a whole bunch of stories by serving others so that, in the end, I could write the book for my great-grandchildren.

"So I did a bunch of volunteer work in the inner city, in Africa, in hospitals, with flying doctors, on suicide crisis lines and with mentally handicapped people. And all the while, I kept reinforcing the notion that as bad as it was for me, there were those who were far worse off. And that consoled and saddened me to a certain extent, but it also gathered these stories.

"That went on for years and eventually I found a way to have a life. Soon after my harsh initiation of coming to Canada, I thought I needed to be more 'Canadian' in order to be accepted, and not get hurt again.

"I got beaten up regularly for sticking up for the fat kids, the underdogs, for being Irish, and so on. I knew that it was dangerous to be myself, to be authentic—or, what we called the 'genuine article' in Ireland.

"So I learned to be a jock, to walk like a hockey player does—tough, buffed up, macho—so I could protect myself from being repeatedly knocked down and beaten up. I learned to fight so well that all my fights lasted only one punch. I forced myself into the Canadian vision of life: to fit in and be accepted—the Canadian dream. (Which is not that different than the American dream, by the way.)

"Either way, it was not MY own dream, based on my genuine self, my own experiences, natural gifts, but some learned, safe, status quo dream where I would not be noticed while pretending to be someone else.

"In my thirties, I felt that I finally had a life. I had created THE life. I had the beautiful house, I had the beautiful wife, I had the beautiful kids. I was making money from my own business; I had the trips and the cars. I had everything I was supposed to have and doing what I was supposed to be doing. I was 'living the dream'.

"Or so I thought.

"Then one morning, I literally was on my way out the door to load up the garden design trucks for my employees and I just fell to my knees. I just started sobbing.

"I had bought into this Canadian dream of 'work hard, don't ask questions, keep your head down' hook, line, and sinker. And suddenly there was nothing inside of me that said yes anymore to that dream.

"I felt utterly disillusioned. I had done everything I was supposed to do to be happy, and yet this had nothing to do with me—the genuine, authentic me.

"On my knees in the driveway that day, I broke down and started sobbing, and it became so clear to me that this was not the way. I just snapped out of it and told myself to get back to what's true for me, true to my own authentic being, true to the person that I had left behind in Ireland.

"I had the first glimpse of this genuineness in me when my first daughter died and I found myself two weeks later at the same James Hillman - Michael Meade gathering that Dave talked about earlier.

Michael Meade asked why everyone was there, and I found myself pushed onto my feet to speak about my daughter's recent death. The floodgates of grief opened in the room, and some two hundred-plus men honoured her passing in an ancient ritual that still touches me deeply twenty-five years later.

"Since then, I have been aiming my life exactly to where it has meaning and purpose. I am now living in the joy, abundance and prosperity of my natural gifts as a wholistic psychotherapist and natural gifts mentor while co-creating NGS as a means to bring each of our 'genuine article-ness' to this wonderful world.

"I have collected many rich stories to tell my grandchildren of treasures hunted and found, distant lands travelled, ordeals with dragons, princesses and princes who found the elixir of love and have lived happily ever after.

"And now people say to me that they want that too. They say, 'I want what you have—or rather, I want my own authentic dream, but with your joy, vitality, intimacy, *connection and meaningful prosperity!'* And I say to them that they can't have my life ... but if they can get the legs on their own dream, then they too can find their version of meaningful vitality, intimacy and prosperity.

"But they must access their genuine natural gifts, and perhaps lean in and work with the various and succinct challenges in their lives in order for these gifts to flourish.

"And so I think you can see why I connect with clients who find themselves in exile in their lives—not living their meaningful life.

"I really understand where they are coming from. I just feel like those people are my people, and that I can mentor them, work with their personality resistances to find their way home to the territory of meaning and purpose.

"I tell them you have got to work with what you've been handed in life—your fate, your wounds, your blessings, your separations, your training, your violations, your family issues, your education, your natural gifts—it all adds up to meaning, a significant and exact knowledge to offer humanity through a meaningful need.

"Then you will have what I have—the life you were meant to be living."

CHAPTER 9:

THE CHRYSALIS STAGE

ASSESSING YOUR OWN GIFTS

*W*e want to answer this call by providing more than just a forum for sharing ideas, more than just bringing back some of the ancient wisdom and connecting it within modern parameters, and putting it all together in a language that people can hear.

We also want to provide simple, practical tools to help bring meaning back into people's lives.

Thus, the Society has developed a Natural Gifts Assessment, which can be accessed from our website at www.naturalgiftssociety.org.

We also offer workshops to give people a first-hand experiential process with others. The learning in these workshops is often more impactful due to the genuine interaction with others.

The Society is a labour of love for us, and none of our Board members are employed by the Society or paid to sit on the Board. We volunteer our time, and we do it gladly, even though we are busy people, and have all kinds of commitments.

But in this moment, we are focusing on the passion in the center, on this little fire in the center, because what we're talking about is really important to us.

We're sharing our hearts with each other and with you.

We are choosing to look at how the world is suffering, and asking ourselves what we can do about it.

It moves us to say that. It's happening in this moment. It's like, *"Okay. There's important work to be done. There's not much time left. And we're rolling up our sleeves and doing it."*

We are grateful to our generous sponsors or donors, both present and future, who are saying, *"Yes, we think this is meaningful, let's put some money or some time into this."*

When we first expose people to our ideas, a common response is one of bewilderment: *"Wow, that's profound— why aren't people talking about this in a bigger way?"*

So we question folks and ask, *"Is this true for you too?*

Are you suffering, or have suffered? Are you bottoming out or done so already?" And we discuss with them the need to go through some sort of transformation to wake up, since our culture continually puts us to sleep again.

When we come together as colleagues at our NGS meetings, we have a ritual that helps us connect with our True Nature. We acknowledge that we have not only each person present, but also each person's gifts.

For example, during our meetings, we have somebody with the gift of hospitality who is really welcoming. *"Welcome, Peter! Welcome, Rebecca! What I have for you is a big hug!"* Or, *"What I have for you is a little treat!"* The gift of hospitality is one of the Natural Gifts.

And when we meet in a circle at another member's house, this gift of hospitality shows up again. They say, *"This is your home, too. You're not a stranger here. You are welcome."* That's a wonderful gift in a large city filled with aloneness and isolation.

We enlist someone with the gift of facilitation to keep our meetings organized and on track.

Several years later, we still follow the ritual of getting into our gifts and escaping from the everyday minutiae such as having had too many business meetings that day or needing to do the laundry, or rushing the kids here and there.

We need to pause, and we need to connect with our deeper self again, and we need to connect with each other.

ASSESSMENT OF NATURAL GIFTS

As stated earlier, we have developed an assessment tool for determining a person's natural gifts, and it's the kind of cognitive approach that people feel comfortable with.

The assessment may show us gifts that we are not aware of, and others may be seed potentials that their family of origin has over and over denounced, such as: *"No, we only have accountants here. Musicians? Those people don't earn a living—forget that!"*

One example is someone's natural gift of music, which hasn't been supported at all, but one day is released in a beautiful and joyful way—a true gift to explore and practice.

There are three parts to the Natural Gifts Assessment. The first part is in the form of a questionnaire. The second is the one-on-one session with a Natural Gift Guide.

This discernment process with the Guide helps determine whether it was one's true self or one's Ego who answered the questionnaire.

This session focuses on the outcome of taking the Assessment, an exploration of one's top four or five natural gifts, and how they resonate with each other, and how they assist each other in forming one's unique purpose.

This discernment process is very important, as it propels one forward into a space where the gifts can be seen in one's current life. It's surprising how they all come together.

The third part is the Manifestation process, which is a separate one-on-one session with the Natural Gift Guide. This session is extremely helpful in finding one's direction with your own unique Natural Gifts.

REBECCA'S STORY

Here is a story from our fourth Board member, Rebecca, about discovering her Natural Gifts through working with a Natural Gifts Guide who facilitated a Natural Gift Assessment for her, and what it meant to her:

"I had been involved with the Natural Gifts Society for almost a year, when I realized I did not know what my own Natural Gifts were. I thought I had a fairly good idea of what I was naturally good at so didn't think I needed to take the Natural Gifts Assessment.

"Then I found out that many people get sidetracked by what they think their gifts are, and what they actually are. This is because the Ego may be the one leading us to think that way.

"Indeed, it may also be the Ego that is taking the initial assessment test, which is why we also have a discernment process to weed out what the Ego wants us to say and what is actually true for us.

"I decided to take the assessment to see if what I

thought were my Natural Gifts actually *were* my gifts, or whether they were perhaps a learned skill or something else that my Ego had conjured up.

"After I took the assessment, a Natural Gift Guide scored it ... and after the discernment process, I was advised of my top six gifts.

"Among these six was the Gift of Encouragement. I didn't even know that encouragement was a Natural Gift and was surprised to learn this. However, it made a lot of sense since I have always been a team player and I often encouraged and supported others, no matter what their goals were.

"What was most interesting though was when the Guide told me that as part of this gift of encouragement, I was also a natural healer. I remember laughing and told her that she was off her rocker, I didn't know anything about healing or how to use my hands to heal, or anything like that. She told me that I was looking at it from a narrow point of view, and that my natural way of healing was in the form of words.

"Wow! That was a huge 'A-ha' moment! In the past, I have found that people naturally come to me to share their challenges and I would very naturally support them to find clarity and come up with their own solutions.

"I didn't see this as a type of 'healing' though. However, from that perspective, it made a lot of sense and I could see how I have helped to 'heal' many through the words I've used. Thus, it was also no surprise to me that I experience the most joy and fulfillment when I coach people.

"This is especially true in the area of relationships, wherein lies my passion. I have always treasured relationships beyond anything else in life, before financial comfort, before material possessions, before my job, and so on. After learning about my Natural Gifts, I understood why I felt so good when I coached people and helped make a difference in their lives.

"I decided to pursue a career as a Relationship Coach. Time and time again, I receive feedback from those I have coached, that I tend to instinctively know not only what to say, but how to say it so that it is effective and helps them produce the results that they want in their relationships, whether it's a relationship with their children, family, friends or significant other.

"And I have to say, giving my gift to this meaningful need has indeed given me immense joy, purpose and fulfillment in my life.

"Thus, I would recommend everyone to discover their gifts so that they too, can live a life with more meaning, joy and fulfillment."

Rebecca is a good example of someone who was called to give her gifts to a meaningful need as a volunteer and ended up getting clearer on her Natural Gifts so she could bring them to her vocation as a Relationship Coach.

EMBRACING OUR YOUTH

The earlier in life we identify our Natural Gifts, the better.

In many cultures, one of the main purposes of a village is to help their youth step into their gifts so that they can stand up and create meaning and purpose for themselves and their community.

Why? It creates a link, like a chain, of strength—all the way around in the village. For example, if you're not delivering your gift of medicine, you may be getting drunk somewhere in some back alley instead.

Meanwhile there is a line of people waiting for the doctor to show up.

And if these people don't get healed, disease and pestilence will spread.

Therefore it's incumbent on us returning to a society that supports the seeing and the nurturing, the deepening and the maintenance, of people being in their gifts.

Because that is how we are going to get better. That is how we're going to create this new world. We need to work collectively to mine the gold in people.

One of Michael and Dave's teachers—a man named Malidoma Some—is a West African shaman who holds a couple of Masters degrees and a PhD. He said, "*The brilliance that's coming into this world through the kids and our grandchildren in this day is so over-the-top, the caliber of brilliance is so over-the-top, the gifts that are coming in are so abundant. But if they're not caught, held, and supported, they will be lost to themselves and the world"*

We believe to some degree that we want to establish some kind of natural structure that can give people a chance to rest into their gifts emotionally, physically, spiritually, in whatever way they can, because our outside culture is putting people on conveyor belts.

We know we can't rely on an educational system that's two hundred years old, one that is not doing a very thorough job in honouring children's gifts, one that is mostly about 'instructors' rather than mentors, one that's primarily about shoving facts in and pulling them out, and seeing how fast they can do that.

Of course there are rare examples of dedicated educators who are really acting as mentors and elders. These are the ones who are on their gift.

Unfortunately in many schools today the main emphasis isn't with bringing youths' innate gifts out in the world. Thus we need to develop the societal structure in place to get the mentorship support, the psychological support, and the emotional support so that these youths can really step up into it.

In our experience, it is a rare person who can step into their gift and walk out the door and say, *"Okay, I'm done. I'm moving on."* It is usually much more of a process.

To begin with, most people cannot do it by themselves

—or rather, they can do it, but they likely won't get the full benefit and maximum return on their efforts. They need someone to guide them through the times when personality resistance, such as fear of change, comes up.

There's another aspect of our Society that echoes the village concept—the fact that we all work together, and there's a wholeness that's achieved by many different individuals coming together in a collective way.

The same goes for the gifts. Each of us has certain gifts, but there are many gifts we don't have. It's the interaction of many people's gifts coming together that creates a greater whole.

As we've stated in Part 1, we also believe that a coherent society, or a coherent village, is very connected with nature, and nature has cycles and seasons. That's why we are skeptical about the kind of model that big businesses employ. Constant growth, as we've stated earlier, isn't sustainable. It's not a natural model.

Thus, when we came together to start the Society, we first created the business side of it, and then we brainstormed a name to describe what we were attempting to achieve with the Society. We came up with the term 'meaningful prosperity'—the prosperity of individuals, of relationships, and of community.

We did some research, and ended up watching a TED talk about this very thing—the need for business to follow nature and have a more cyclical pattern, without ending up with runaway systems that are unsustainable.

Talk about synchronicity! And so we knew we were on the right track.

We immediately felt that something bigger than us was watching over us and helping us. And in creating the small community of a Non Profit Society, we were in fact re-imagining society as a whole, because we believe it's a process of nature and culture coming together.

We believe we have to model what Gandhi espoused, *"To be the change we want to see in the world."*

And part of our vision is to learn the technology, the art and the science of how we can build a different way to be engaged in the business of soul making, the business of bringing people to a meaningful life.

YOUTH LIVING WITH MEANING AND PURPOSE

There has been much said about so-called Indigo children, and we all probably know some young person who fits that description. We know examples of instances where the gift of compassion seems to happen at birth. There is the story of a seven year-old Ontario boy called Ryan Hreljac who listened intently to his teacher telling his classroom that there were children in Africa who have no clean drinking water.

Immediately Ryan said. *"So, what can I do about it?"*

The teacher was shocked because she didn't expect that response from the children. She was interested in educating them about the facts. But he was undaunted. "*Well*," he said, "*I will send them my allowance.*"

No doubt the teacher—and also everyone else in the class—smiled and didn't take his remark seriously. But he started a fund, and raised money through a foundation called the Ryan's Well Foundation, and sure enough, his first well was built at Angolo Public School in northern Uganda.

To date, he and friends have raised millions of dollars and have completed over five hundred projects, bringing access to clean water and sanitation to over seven hundred and fifty thousand people in sixteen developing countries. One of our members was privileged to meet Ryan, this boy with the gift of compassion.

We know of several examples like that, where people don't take someone seriously simply because they present themselves in a young package at the time, but the gifts of compassion or wisdom will take different forms. Many of us hear a child speak words of wisdom that are way beyond their years.

In British Columbia there is a young man named Simon Jackson. Also at the age of seven, he saw his first wild bear while on a camping trip with his parents. This ignited his interest in bears, and at the age of thirteen he began a campaign to save the spirit bear, found mainly in an area known as the Great Bear Rainforest, on the central coast north of Vancouver Island.

He spread his message by taking a slide show around the province to schools and anyone else that would listen. That campaign has lasted for over two decades already, rallying more than six million people including heads of state, rock stars and environmentalists, to save these bears from extinction by protecting their habitat.

We would say people like Ryan and Simon are examples of youth who already have the seeds of 'the elder within' and perfect illustrations of people sharing their gifts with a meaningful need.

Our fifth NGS Board Member, Anne Marie, was blessed to work with youth to help them uncover their gifts in a program called Katimavik. She later discovered her healing gift and now is a Natural Gifts Guide.

ANNE MARIE'S STORY

"After a chronic, severe health issue thwarted my progression in a corporate management track, I took time away and created a U-turn in my life.

"When headaches caused me to severely limit my activities, foods, and focus, as a last resort I turned to alternative healing modalities. These modalities clearly assisted me in regaining my health.

"My intuition played a major part of this U-turn, as I

had spent a lot of time in my 'headache' space—basically a meditative state—and during a reiki and shiatsu session, I heard a seemingly internal voice tell me I needed to learn how to do this.

"Heeding this voice, I took all levels of reiki energy healing, and later completed a Natural Vision Educator program.

"My early work life had given me a lot of fun experiences working with youth at their time of transitioning from mum and dad's oversight into their own paths, and I listened and coached them towards their passions and interests.

"This national program was extremely useful for youth at that time, a vehicle to help them find their passions and gifts, experiencing opportunities most would never have.

"The next step for me was with a corporate traffic safety youth leadership program, utilizing my administrative and leadership gifts in high schools and co-creating conferences and programs.

"I believe these fostering and mentoring opportunities were an important step for these young folks, who volunteered their time and gained so much knowledge about themselves; their likes, dislikes, their uniqueness and where they absolutely thrived.

"Fast forward to the present. Having heard of the idea of natural gifts, I undertook an assessment, which—through a discernment process—validated my wide range of interests and instances where I felt whole.

"I had uncovered my gifts, two of which were the gifts of Healing and Administration.

"I leapt at the idea of working with a group of like-minds in forming the Natural Gifts Society, and soon found myself researching, developing, and co-creating the questionnaire and program for the Natural Gifts Assessment.

"This continues to be very enjoyable, and since this work utilizes my gifts of administration and healing and service, it also feels meaningful.

"As a Natural Gifts Assessment Guide, I'm enjoying helping others uncover their unique sets of natural gifts, and the discernment and coaching process is delightful when I see others get to that 'aha' moment of finding their place among their gifts.

"A recent client shared with me that when her top five gifts were uncovered, she was not too surprised, as she could see all of them at times in her life.

"However, what ended up being the surprise was how she now saw and experienced these gifts synergistically, and her actions and ways of doing things suddenly made more sense.

"This group of natural gifts became a foundation for her."

FROM CRISIS TO OPPORTUNITY

From the stories of our Board members, we see that most of them have undergone a kind of midlife crisis and rebirth. The crisis became an initiation and opportunity for them to turn inward toward their wound until it became a womb to birth their new life of meaning and purpose.

We can see that prior to the initiatory phase each of them got caught in the *busyness* of adult life, juggling all the responsibilities that establishing a career or raising a family entails.

In the process, they each got somewhat lost—until they found mentors and community to help them identify their Natural Gifts.

Coming together and supporting each other ends the isolation, loneliness and meaninglessness that modern culture propagates.

Together they are becoming a part of the solution by directing some of their time and means to help awaken youths to their Natural Gifts, help middle-aged adults, like themselves, wake up to their opportunity for a life of meaning and purpose and help seniors become elders.

ELDERSHIP

Part of our mission is to answer the call of eldership and bring together ancient pathways and new beginnings.

Today's youth are especially in need of guidance, with

too many of them feeling so off-track that they have no idea which way to go. Many don't trust the boomers; boomers have used up everything. There's nothing left. As costs sky-rocket, even buying a house is out of reach for this group. They're upset that there's no culture to lean onto; so they're leaning onto each other. We are turning into a sibling culture. They are all going to raise themselves.

American activist and author Robert Bly wrote a book about sibling societies, and it's not pretty. The book argues that many modern adults face difficulties caused by an inability to reach full maturity, and discusses the consequences this has for the societies in which they live.

That's why we believe the call that we're answering, to some degree, is eldership. It's a mammoth task that we hope to achieve, but it's not going to be for lack of trying.

There is wisdom that needs to be shared, and it has to be relevant to now. It can't be Greek wisdom. It can't be Irish wisdom. It can't be ancient Taoist wisdom. It can't be Dutch wisdom. It has to be relevant for now.

There are two prongs of wisdom that our teachers talk about. One—there is the *wisdom of guidance*, of being able to guide somebody in his or her life. Call that a mentor, call that a therapist, call that a friend, whatever that is, it is wise counselling and meaningful guidance that is relevant, accurate, and just for you personally.

The other prong is a *lyric wisdom*, a spontaneous wisdom, and a wisdom that we feel inside our bones. It's a wisdom that comes from who we are, and it's a wisdom that is like a sound that starts to resonate and creates the music of who we really are.

When we're in that gift, we hear that music. The meaningful life is the dance of that music.

And so, eldership is about leadership, about really seeing your kids, and knowing who they are, and caring about who they are. It's about watching over them when they become teenagers and start drinking their faces off or doing something stupid, and reminding them who they are. That's our job as an elder! That's *eldership*.

We also use eldership amongst ourselves in the Society, to keep each other in order if it should be necessary. It's our job to say to someone, *"Hey, John Doe, a little too strong there, can you dial it down a bit?"* And we do it coming from a place of altruism, caring and compassion; a place of wanting only the best for the other; a place of eldership.

Eldership is about blessing; it's about wisdom. We, as elders, have to stitch together ancient pathways into a new beginning. This is our time. We have to see that this Society that we've started is a big part of finding a way to bring new things together—it's what we need today, in terms of nature and culture, past and present or past and future, male and female, old and new—these roles all coming together.

It has to be relevant for *now*. It's got to be something

that is not only relevant, but something that connects with people—especially young people. It has to be relevant for your children, your grandchildren and your great-grandchildren.

It has to answer that call. That's what eldership is. We need to start creating that legacy now, and put something in place that our great- great- great-grandchildren, even seven generations from now, will still be living on.

THE ELDER WITHIN

Shakespeare wrote, '*All of life's a stage*' and indeed we all drop through the mystery onto the stage of life through the womb, and we go along merrily and all of a sudden at age seven or sixteen or later, life gives us a blow and there is an initiatory moment.

If we get help from an elder or a mentor, we are seen and we are blessed, and we can shift into the next level of our growth—on to the next scene of our life, to follow the Shakespeare analogy.

If we are not seen, our growth is stunted, and even though we move along in life chronologically, we remain behind spiritually, emotionally and psychologically.

There's a story that we'd like to share about a senior's home that we visited a couple of times, doing drumming, sing-alongs and storytelling.

One day Dave heard that the son of a resident, who

was our main contact there, had just passed away. She had, called and said, *"I really want to come to your drum circle and sing-along, but my youngest son just died..."* and so we were both crying on the phone.

He had done four tours of military duty in Afghanistan, the last two almost consecutively as a human intelligence operator. He had come home from each tour severely traumatized. He had sought professional help a number of times and with each failure, it seems he grew to believe there was no help. He dealt with some of his pain by self-medicating with alcohol.

Meanwhile his wife became pregnant, but it seems when she told him the news, the thought of harming or even killing his child and wife, while still in the grip of PSTD, was more than he could bear. Out of love, he believed it would be better to commit suicide, in order to keep them safe.

Our contact, a creative white teacher fell in love with a black African man, while both were completing their degrees at UBC. Two years later, they married in Kenya and over the years had four beautiful children, now grown up.

We decided we would call our friends from the Natural Gifts Society and Soultime Express and go to celebrate his life with her at the seniors' home. She said, *"That's so wonderful—my son would have liked to have his life celebrated; that's what is done in Africa! It will also help me to break the news to the other residents here."*

So we got at least a dozen people together and went over there with African drums and percussion instruments. She was so glad to see us. She had written a children's book called 'The Gift' which is all about what we are talking about, and she wanted to use it to honour her son. She asked Dave to be the storyteller because she was so upset she couldn't read it aloud.

One of the characters in her story is a wise elder, so we got her to play that part and she had just a few lines to read. There was a 'chorus' made up of all the people— the seniors included, who were all watching this. All of our friends were there with their drums and singing, and it was a really meaningful experience for everyone.

Fast forward almost six months later, and the child was born. Again, we showed up, this time to welcome the birth of her grandson. She asked us to tell a story, and we weren't sure what story to tell so Dave just made one up.

Pointing to a big exit sign at one end of the room, he said, "*Well, your son left through that exit sign over there, and went into the Great Mystery. We don't really know what's on the other side of that door. Most call it death, but let's just call it the Mystery.*

"*So in Africa, that would make him an ancestor. And now, on the other side of the room, there's another entrance doorway ... and this child has just dropped through from the Mystery onto the stage of life.*"

It just so happened that the twelve-year old daughter

of one of our members was sitting on that side too, and on the other side—the exit—sat two women who were about a hundred years old, and everyone else of different ages were between those two extremes.

Initiation happens more than once in our lifetime.

These challenging times invite us into the next greatest passage of our life, so by the time we are over there closer to the exit door, we are not just an older person—a senior—we are in fact an elder, and this is what this friend/mother has been blossoming into for many years now.

And so we were there to witness, bless and greet this woman who was stepping into the next dimension of her elderhood via the wound of coping with the loss of her son and the birth of her grandchild six months later.

Joy and sorrow became the tag team for the maturing of an elder. The seniors were quite moved by having been witnesses and participants in this event. They asked us how much we were going to charge their centre. We told them we don't charge. They were surprised and said, *"Everybody else that comes to entertain us charges a fee! We can't afford many groups and wish we could have more."*

We said, *"This isn't about entertainment—it's about answering the call, the call to building a soulful community."*

ELDERS VS OLDERS

- Elders don't have to be in their nineties; Olders are old long before they reach the half-way point

- Elders are rascally and teeming with story and wonderment; Olders seem to be attached to suffering

- Elders have joy and a wicked sense of humour; Olders simply don't smile a lot

- Elders are fiercely gentle with buckets of patience; Olders are rough in all the wrong places

- Elders bring people Home; Olders live in exile, disconnected from a true life of deep sustenance

- Elders can bless; Olders end up cursing

- Elders really "see" people's gold and gifts; Olders "look" for deficiencies and problems

- Elders are very interested in what interests youth; Olders are too busy for the dreams of the youth

- Elders are continually arrested by beauty; Olders are arrested in a beauty that has long past its' prime

- Creativity flourishes around Elders; Olders don't get what it's like to live with creativity

CHAPTER 10:

TRANSFORMATION BUTTERFLY

WHERE IS THE VILLAGE?

*M*ichael recalls being at a leadership conference many years ago.

He was the youngest guy there, in his early thirties at the time, and he remembers looking around at one point and watching about three hundred older people chatting on and on about this and that, and he got so frustrated that he grabbed the talking stick, stepped into the circle, and went up one side and down the other, shouting at them, frustrated because none of them were looking down—they were not seeing the youth.

"You guys are all navel-gazers!" he shouted. *"What are you doing?"*

"What about the young people? What about us" What about me!" he yelled.

One of the delegates to that conference was a man in a wheelchair who was a 'paid mentor' and looked after several children of US Senators in Washington D.C. He was a very smart man, with a PhD in Philosophy, and he said that moment changed the whole focus of the men's gathering. He said the fact that this young man could stand up and really lay it out to them and didn't hold anything back, was what changed everything.

Michael got a note from him soon afterwards, a beautiful letter from this man who was paid to mentor the children of all these powerful people; a letter that commended him on his courage. Talk about being seen!

In psychology they use the term 'mirroring' to describe essentially the same process, but we much prefer 'being seen' or 'being blessed'. Really being deeply seen is a much, much richer term. The emphasis is on witnessing and reflecting back the youth's Natural Gifts!

James Hillman said that if you are still struggling with your father, ask yourself what temple he was serving in. He said in yoga there are four schools or four temples, and your father may have served in a different temple to the one you are serving in.

You need to find the elders and mentors of your temple, or else you will forever be complaining about what you never got from your father.

You need a village.

You need wise elders like James Hillman, Michael Meade and Malidoma Somé.

Meade has worked in prison with youths, he was in the Vietnam War and spent time in solitary confinement—and his gift of language is just mind blowing.

At the age of four Malidoma was kidnapped by Jesuit missionaries, to be raised in their boarding school and given a Western education. By taking away children, the missionaries were attempting to convert black Africans to Christianity. Malidoma believes it was his destiny to come to a Western audience in friendship and tell them about his experience of being torn away from his people by Westerners.

But before he could communicate with his people, he had to undergo a process of 'relearning'—a month-long Dagara 'initiation process'.

These two men who have experienced extreme torture in their own way, are elegant examples that out of the greatest wound can come the greatest blessing.

And, just like the butterfly needs the struggle of drying and strengthening its wings in order to fly after coming out of the cocoon, so too the suffering is an important component of becoming a mentor and an elder.

One final thing about the need for a village.

To get back to the cocoon, it's really fascinating what

happens there. From some of our studies we understand that the cocoon itself has to be strong, and if it's not strong enough—for example if it's too thin—the transformation won't happen. In fact, the caterpillar may die.

So it really requires a tight enough community, a village, and that's one of the problems we find today—to try to do it all in the therapist's office isn't enough.

We need friends, we need circles and we need a community of people that become our extended cocoon to help us go through this transformational process.

VILLAGE BUILDING

We provide the form for and often facilitate Natural Gifts Circles and other events to foster a sense of community.

We also provide volunteer opportunities for folks who want to be more involved with like-minded people engaged in making a difference in their community and the world.

TRAINING PROGRAMS

YOUTH

We currently do some volunteering in schools and our Natural Gifts Circles so youth can identify their Natural Gifts early on in life.

YOUNG ADULTS

We have an assessment available and offer mentorship for young adults struggling with quarter life crisis due to lack of direction.

MIDLIFE

We have assessments available and offer mentorship for middle-aged adults struggling with midlife crisis as a result of lack of meaning and purpose.

SENIORS

We visit centers where seniors are receptive to our message. We also offer mentorship for seniors who are ready to undergo initiation and training into elderhood.

BUSINESS PEOPLE

We have initiated Natural Gifts Circles for Business people so they have a venue and method to support each other for inspiration to live with greater meaning and purpose. The dream is to bring Natural Gifts Assessments into the work place to have more people living in the joy of giving their gifts at work. Imagine the low turnover if all your employees loved their work!

NATURAL GIFTS GUIDES

We are developing training to recognize and support the gifts in those who are called to becoming a Natural

Gifts Guide to lead Natural Gifts Circle and facilitate Natural Gift Assessments in order to help others identify their Natural Gifts.

NATURAL GIFTS MENTORS

We are developing training to recognize and develop the gifts of counseling and coaching professionals who can help people identify their Natural Gifts and are qualified to help them work through their personality resistances so they can manifest their gifts.

GROWING OUR CIRCLE OF INFLUENCE

We now have begun to move outward and spread our message. Starting with regular Natural Gifts Circles, conducting weekend workshops, and on to training folks to become guides and mentors and elders, ensures that our work can become a legacy.

We can also see how our stewardship can be of great value to others who are in advisory or mentorship positions. Coaches, counsellors, therapists, and others can benefit from insights into accessing people's inner gifts and can be encouraged to use them in a meaningful way.

If we can develop a simple technology for them, they can use these tools to help them to essentially be spiritual guides. You don't have to be a priest or guru to do this; as long as you have the necessary Natural Gifts and training, you can become a guide or mentor to help others identify their gifts.

The Natural Gifts Society will grow by extrapolating our work, sharing our knowledge, continuously gaining wisdom, and by organizing it all in a way that members can use it, learn from it and share it.

There are basically three aspects of what we are aiming at doing. The first is to provide the environment— physical as well as virtual—so that people can share. The second is to organize our growing body of knowledge and research into an accessible form. The third is the community—and the more the community grows, the more they will themselves be spreading and perpetuating this path of awareness of gifts.

Another aspect of spreading our message and our influence is—as one of our colleagues put it—to 'entice people into our meaningful mall'.

In today's commercialized society it's impossible not to be aware of the relentless and pervasive marketing machine that is pulling the people into malls everywhere, including of course, the online malls. The advertising agencies are experts at creating a need and a desire, even when there wasn't one before.

We need to be the David to Goliath, and find ways of bringing people to our door by offering some valuable and useful enticements, like finding themselves. Like getting greater meaning and purpose.

We also call it 'bringing people home'.

We recognize that there are some obstacles in the way of us growing the Society as we envision—initially lack of resources, time and energy—but we are confident that we can overcome those obstacles and continue to develop enough quality programs for the volumes of people that will join us.

As we've said before—there's a cry out there already, and we believe that once the word gets out, the people will come. It's like anything else.

One of our members was a pioneer in bringing yoga to Vancouver, and at first people were skeptical and even contemptuous, but just look at how it has grown, into a huge movement!

The same goes for meditation. These days meditation can be found in every walk of life, in so many different forms.

And so we firmly believe there will come a time when people will be able to say, "*I need to get down into my gifts. I just need to go down and sit by that fire at the NGS. I just need to go and hang out with them, because something happens when I sit there.*

"*On a cellular level, that's why I love to just hang out.*"

In the future we know there will be many Natural Gifts Circles. We also have targeted having multiple centers around the world.

It's obviously a big vision. But even a thousand mile journey begins with the first step.

SPENDING TIME WITH NATURE

Many wise writers and philosophers like Walt Whitman and Henry David Thoreau revered nature. So, not surprisingly, we like to take people into natural surroundings to help them connect with themselves.

Both in our capacity as Natural Gifts Society founders as well as in our private lives, we often work with those who are not consciously 'spiritual'; if we take them out into nature or the wilderness, they suddenly slow down.

They're not waking up to an alarm, and they eat when they're hungry, not just because it's mealtime.

And when they go to bed they sleep very soundly, because they've been out all day hiking or doing something physical in the fresh air.

Gradually they are able to feel a natural rhythm that they are a part of.

They soon begin to realize that they are not living their natural rhythm in the city. There's a different kind of rhythm in the concrete jungle, one that dances to an egoist rhythm.

But once they get into the wilderness, they start to slow down, and they start to feel like they are part of nature, part of the wilderness.

Pulitzer Prize winning poet Mary Oliver expresses the experience of nature wonderfully in her poem *Wild Geese*:

"Whoever you are, no matter how lonely,
the world offers itself to your imagination,
calls to you like the wild geese, harsh and exciting --
over and over announcing your place
in the family of things."

Spend some time out in nature, and all of a sudden you really feel like you belong. *"I'm part of this wildness. Some part of me is wild."* There's something beautiful in the wildness of nature that is our own beauty that is our own untamed part of us. And that's part of our true nature.

And so, part of our challenge is, how do we put this in a form that's going to meet people who are unaware or shut down?

We would love to help them move into their gifts. But often we see them in a pretty wounded state. There is no judgment in saying that—in fact, we have all been wounded at some time or the other. In fact, a couple of our colleagues refer to themselves as 'wounded healers'.

LOVING THE QUESTIONS

These are big existential questions. Very few people have the courage to stop and say, *"Well, who am I then? What is my purpose?"*

The poet Rilke has another great line around that. He wrote,

"Don't search for the answers, which could not be given to you now, because you would not be able to live them. And the point is, to live everything. Live the questions now. Perhaps then, someday far in the future, you will gradually, without even noticing it, live your way into the answer."

The questions will take you on a quest towards the answer.

For some people, those questions may seem like dangerous questions, because they will transform your life ... because when you ask, "Who am I?" in all sincerity, you may come up with a confusing answer, and that could be the beginning of a sudden big change that is about to happen.

A good technique for exploring questions like these are to keep addressing each answer you come up with another question—for example:

"Who am I"?

"I'm a therapist."

"Okay, but who am I really?"

"Well, I'm a husband..."

"Sure I am, but who am I really?"

Get the picture? You keep going deeper and deeper, and the veils keep being removed for a deeper and deeper discussion.

THE NGS EQUATION REVISITED

We originally set out to create a simple model of the five aspects of what we are trying to achieve. The scientifically minded will no doubt be pleased to see an equation, while the more spiritually minded will hopefully also find it pleasing.

There's a great deal of research now in neuroscience, focusing on the differences between the right hemisphere and the left hemisphere of the brain, as well as how they work together synergistically. Psychotherapist and author Iain McGilchrist has done some wonderful TED talks on this, and one of the simple images that he uses really sums it up for us. For the left hemisphere we picture the sharp end of a wedge, and the right hemisphere is the widened part.

Then he uses the analogy of a bird, and says it uses the left hemisphere to zero in and peck at a seed. It's used for focus. The right hemisphere, on the other hand, can be ever alert for danger and the big picture. And so both hemispheres have an important function.

The bird is another universal symbol of the soul. We need to see the bigger picture and zero in on the important details.

Today's culture has evolved in such a way that we are dominant with regard to the left hemisphere, and so get hung up on the wrong details and we tend to overvalue the people with the gifts of the left hemisphere.

The result is that a lot of our instructional institutions and our corporations are very left-hemisphere dominant. Our yang currency reflects this!

And where there is dominance on the left, then the right brain—and its intuition and creativity—often goes into the arts, or areas like that. The result is that we have a real economic imbalance based on that.

There's a lot of talk these days about the brain being located in the head and the body. In the head, there are three brains—the reptilian brain, the mammalian brain, and the pre-frontal lobes.

But within the body itself, there's also what is referred to as the 'gut-brain'. As we stated earlier, both the heart and gut are important centers of neural activity.

We believe that in order to know what you love, you have to be in touch with your heart, and your gut has incredible intelligence to guide you instinctively as well.

And so, when we work with people, it can be quite a transformational experience when they have mostly been identified with their left hemisphere (and the collection of 'selves' that live there!) and have been judgmental about people who are right-hemisphere dominant.

In a way, their strong judgment often comes about because they've disowned those parts of themselves.

Such people are either attracted to them as their opposite, or they may be judgmental about them.

Or vice versa—people who are very right-hemisphere dominant often have negative judgment about left-hemisphere dominant people.

As we evolve as whole human beings, however, we recognize that if we can have access to both, our right and left hemispheres, as well as our heart and gut, our full body and all the gifts that we have, then we can be more of a fully-functional human being.

MAP = TN + EQ + NG – PR + MN

Let's review our equation one last time—however, let's look at it from a slightly different model following a simple A, B, C, D, and E structure that we refer to as aspects of our 'MAP'.

'A' IS FOR EXPANDED AWARENESS

That's part of our True Nature. (TN)

'B' IS FOR BEING

Being aware of our Essential Qualities (EQ), and the fact that they come from our very being. *The Ground of Being* is a Christian mystical term; the acorn has to drop down into the ground of being.

'C' IS FOR CONSCIOUSNESS

We need to be conscious of our Essential Qualities (EQ)

and Natural Gifts (NG). Some people call our consciousness our soul.

'D' IS FOR DISCERNMENT

Being able to discern what the Personality Resistance (PR) is that is blocking us from being aware of or giving away our gifts. In essence, we need a more transparent ego and for the ego to get on board for the service of giving our gifts.

'E' IS FOR EVOLVEMENT

This involves giving your gift to a Meaningful Need. (MN)

So, in order for anyone to have M.A.P.—Meaning And Purpose—in their lives, they need TN + EQ + NG - PR + MN.

That's what connects us to the world.

It's what brings our gifts, our soul, into the world— for soulful relationships, soulful work and a soulful life.

We find the MAP expresses our concepts in a simple language that most people can understand, while also honouring the depth of all the traditions we've studied.

We have an ego-personality for a reason.

And the reason that we've found is that it develops self-reflective consciousness.

We have been given free will, but it's not really free unless we know that we have the choice to use it.

Once we become more conscious we are able to have an "*Aha!*" moment, and realize that we can overcome our negative past and surrender into our fundamental being.

This being unfolds naturally toward who we are meant to become.

THE BLOSSOMED ROSE

In order to speak about the soul we need to reach for metaphor. It is said that the heart is the seat of the soul. In Sufism, the rose is the symbol of the heart. If it's open, it gives off its fragrance.

And in the whirling dervish ceremony descended from the time of Rumi, before they begin, they spray the mist of essential rose oil all over the room. And it's a symbol for the scent of the Beloved.

One Sufi master said, "*If the teacher of love is like a blossomed rose, then what the student is recognizing is the potential of their own roseness, they have the rosebud inside of them that recognizes a reflection of their own unique blossomed self in the teacher.*"

When they see the teacher, it's like the rosebud of their true self—like our acorn—starts to crack open. They desire the light of the sun, because they're seeing the potential of who they are to become eventually.

The true teacher reflects our essence back to us.

They also need to hang around with the teacher for

a while, to learn things like, "*What is the fragrance of my particular rose? How am I going to unfold this into the world?*"

Our wish for you is that you become, truly, a blossomed rose and give your unique fragrance of beauty to the world.

The Sufi poet Hafiz describes it beautifully in his poem *It Felt Love* in the book *The Gift* by Daniel Ladinsky:

How
Did the rose
Ever open its heart

And give to this world
All its
Beauty?

It felt the encouragement of light
Against its
Being,

Otherwise,
We all remain

Too
Frightened.

Cultivating your Natural Gifts is like cultivating a nourishing garden. As we care for our garden our seeds start to sprout and blossom. Occasionally we will have some weeding and pruning to do. Over time our garden begins to flourish, feeding us, and others.

Thank you for joining us in this soulful journey from acorn to mighty oak tree: from caterpillar to beautiful butterfly, and from closed rose to one that is opening to give its delightful fragrance and beauty.

May your journey be blessed and fruitful!

And so, in closing, may you see this book as a beautiful gift from the Natural Gifts Society to your soul. We hope we have been able to give you insights and some inspiration to find your true self and share it with the world in a meaningful way.

Until we meet again!

ABOUT THE AUTHORS

DAVE WALI WAUGH, RPC

Dave is Co-Founder and Vice-President of the Natural Gifts Society. He loves to inspire people of all ages to awaken to and live their Natural Gifts through the arts of storytelling and wholistic process.

As a Wholistic Psychotherapist and Natural Gifts Mentor, he is passionate about designing wholistic programs and facilitating processes that assist clients in healing, transformation and evolution.

He finds that it is very fulfilling to journey together and

witness the people he works with gradually awaken to a renewed sense of vitality in body, emotion, mind, heart and soul.

With this renewal, it is meaningful to witness them cultivate more intimate relationships while discovering the joy of living with a deeper sense of meaning and purpose.

Dave can also be reached at www.davewaugh.net

MICHAEL TALBOT KELLEY, MA, RCC

Michael is Co-Founder and President of the Natural Gifts Society. He is a Vancouver-based Wholistic Psychotherapist, Natural Gifts Mentor and Spiritual Counselor. He shares his time between his private practice in Vancouver and the Chopra Addiction and Wellness Center in Squamish, BC.

Michael has more than 30 years of experience working in the field of healing beginning with a volunteer stint as a medical assistant in Africa. On returning to Canada, he was involved in opening a Spiritual Healing Centre in the 1980's that was on the forefront of providing support services for those suffering with HIV-AIDS. Michael went on to get a Masters in Psychology, and brings a breadth of training and practical life-experience to his practice.

Michael's work honours the individual and he believes that no one is a problem to be solved, we are all mysteries to be embraced. He helps his clients shift their focus to bringing their Natural Gifts, wholeness and imagination into balance with many of the challenges in our modern world.

For more information about Michael's work visit www. michaeltalbotkelly.com

PETER CHEUNG

Peter is one of the Directors of the NGS. The reason he loves the concept of discovering your Natural Gifts and then living within them to create more purpose and meaning in your life is because he personally went through such a process himself.

He spent over twenty years in the field of technology and while it was exciting, it did not give him a sense of fulfillment. Then he discovered that his gifts of Entrepreneurship and Leadership were to support others and create a positive difference to their lives.

When he changed life careers and applied that concept to his work life, the magic started to appear. He saw the difference he was making in his own life as well as others, and today it feels great to live in alignment with his purpose.

His goal is to support as many as he can to discover their Natural Gifts so that they too, can live with purpose, meaning and passion.

REBECCA CHEUNG

Rebecca is one of the Directors of the Natural Gifts Society. She is a proud mother who loves spending time with her family and the love of her life, Peter. Her passion is anything to do with children and helping people in obtaining the relationships of their dreams.

When she heard about the Natural Gifts Society, she immediately resonated with how it could serve the children of the world. She loved the idea that if children were to discover their Natural Gifts early on in life and receive the ongoing support in order to live their lives according to their Gifts, it would lead to a life filled with meaning, purpose and passion.

Imagine a world where mid-life crises are a thing of the past because all children have learned to live on purpose right from the beginning! Until that day comes, Rebecca will continue to do what she can to spread the word .... because our children are the future, and we are all worth it.

ANNE MARIE KONAS

Anne Marie is co-founder and Secretary/Treasurer of the Natural Gifts Society. She often follows flashes of intuition in making changes in her life. She balances her main gifts of Administration, Healing and Service with administrative contracts and healing work with clients.

She is also a Natural Gifts Guide and offers Natural Gifts Assessments through the website www.naturalgiftssociety. org.

Anne Marie particularly enjoys working with individuals who are open to self-discovery, and who are ready to make changes in their lives in a positive, empowering and meaningful way.